God's *FORMULA* *FOR* FINANCIAL FREEDOM

RODNEY A. BARBETTO, JR.

Trilogy Christian Publishers
A Wholly Owned Subsidiary of Trinity Broadcasting Network
2442 Michelle Drive
Tustin, CA 92780
Copyright © 2024 by Rodney A. Barbetto, Jr.
Scripture quotations marked ESV are taken from the English Standard Version. Copyright © 2001 by Crossway, a publishing ministry of Good News Publishers. Used by permission. All rights reserved.
Scripture quotations marked NRSVA are taken from the New Revised Standard Version Bible: Anglicised Edition, copyright © 1989, 1995 the Division of Christian Education of the National Council of the Churches of Christ in the United States of America. Used by permission. All rights reserved.
Scripture quotations marked NLT are taken from the New Living Translation. Copyright © 1996, 2004, 2015 by Tyndale House Foundation. Used by permission of Tyndale House Publishers, Inc., Carol Stream, Illinois 60188. All rights reserved.
All rights reserved, including the right to reproduce this book or portions thereof in any form whatsoever.
For information, address Trilogy Christian Publishing
Rights Department, 2442 Michelle Drive, Tustin, CA 92780.
Trilogy Christian Publishing/ TBN and colophon are trademarks of Trinity Broadcasting Network.
For information about special discounts for bulk purchases, please contact Trilogy Christian Publishing.
Trilogy Disclaimer: The views and content expressed in this book are those of the author and may not necessarily reflect the views and doctrine of Trilogy Christian Publishing or the Trinity Broadcasting Network.

10 9 8 7 6 5 4 3 2 1
Library of Congress Cataloging-in-Publication Data is available.
ISBN 979-8-89333-598-9
ISBN 979-8-89333-599-6 (ebook)

Dedication

This book is dedicated to you, the reader.

I am excited to see you become financially free!

DISCLAIMER

God's Formula for Financial Freedom is not intended as a substitute for the advice of a licensed attorney, accountant, financial advisor, or any other certified financial professional.

Acknowledgements

First off, I would like to thank my Lord and Savior Jesus Christ for leading me and guiding me in writing this book, for without Him, I can do nothing. I also want to thank my dad for teaching me about finances starting at a very young age. I would like to thank Jesse Duplantis for his influence through his messages on finances as they were the starting blocks for me in writing this book. From there, I was able to further study God's Word and start my own financial journey. I would also like to thank Jerry Savelle for his preaching of faith in regard to finances. Lastly, I would like to thank Joel Osteen for his words of hope, love, and inspiration which allowed me to step out in faith to write this book and for letting me know that writing a book is possible. These three have been pillars of love and hope in my life that go beyond words and into actions.

Table of Contents

Prologue 11

Introduction 17

Part One: Spiritual Foundation. 29

Chapter 1: A Day with God 31

Chapter 2: Give to God 37

Chapter 3: Alms and Firstfruits 45

Chapter 4: Above All, Tithe. 49

Chapter 5: Seeding and Using Talents 53

Chapter 6: Bible Verses become Statements of Faith. . . 65

Part Two: Financial Structure. 71

Chapter 7: Meet the Financial You 73

Chapter 8: More Than One Kind of Savings 81

Chapter 9: Eliminate Credit Card Debt. 89

A. Avoid the Credit Card Trap 94

B. Before Chapter 13 99

C. Bankruptcy 102

Chapter 10: Ways to Make Money 105

Chapter 11: How to Allocate. 117

Conclusion 123

Testimonials 127

About the Author. 131

Endnotes 133

Prologue

My parents gave me the groundwork for *God's Formula for Financial Freedom*. Throughout my life they shared their passions for investing, public speaking, helping others, and Christian living. My father worked for the IRS, and after work he studied the stock market. He bought the *Wall Street Journal* daily and followed it closely. My mother was a herbologist and iridologist who regularly attended and presented at conventions. She explained her herbs and treatments to individuals and groups of all sizes. Because she had MS and had found relief with herbs and holistic medicines, she was delighted to share her knowledge and healing with others. I sometimes witnessed the thanks she received from those she helped, and it was so rewarding that I wanted to give in a similar way. Then as the disease weakened her, I gradually began to do presentations in her place.

At home, my parents were an example of Christian living. With them, I attended church, Sunday school, and numerous other Christian events. They also sent their children—me included—to Christian schools. They shared their religious and secular lives with me. By the age of nine, I knew how to pray some simple prayers and how to track stocks. Under my mother's instruction, I grew to confidently give presentations and speak to groups.

I also enjoyed the benefits of their work and endeavors. My father put together a financial safety net that provided security for our family as well as his parents. We were not overindulged, but we were privileged not to know real need. The safety net gave us a lot of confidence. We had all the necessities and some extra things. I was blessed to feel loved and cared for. I think more families—you and your family—can enjoy that same financial safety and the confidence it instills.

My school life was not smooth. I was unable to read until almost eighth grade and struggled to read far into high school. I was in special classes for most of my elementary schooling. I was bullied, teased, ostracized. For some reason, in sixth grade, I remember I had had enough and thought I would be better off dead. I still clearly remember feeling as though "Christ" or "God" spoke to me and said, "I will always be with you," and I found or was "given" the strength to go on. As I reflect now, I know that my home training and Christian education made it possible to "hear" that reassuring voice.

In school, I always had to work extra hard to do my academic work, and I was completely left out socially. Because of my own experience, I will always have empathy for those who are segregated and made to feel "less than." On the other hand, my scholastic problems made my time with my father special. My dad treated me as competent, and I learned how to invest in the market. As a child, I was doing something many adults cannot do. I did love

PROLOGUE

following the stock market with my father, and I love it to this day. From the age of six onward, I tracked my favorite stocks and as soon as I was old enough, I made some purchases. Until recently, I had so little money to invest that while I consistently chose winners, I made hardly any money. Still, I enjoyed it.

While I was not good at school, I could handle employment! Even just out of high school, I had two jobs, as a server and a bank teller. For two years, I worked hard and saved. I continued to go to church. Then I met my wife, and we had two children. The bank for which I was working closed and there were layoffs, of which I was one. I quickly found a new and better job in another state. Even though I had a promotion and a little savings from the time I was single, I now had a family and my financial responsibilities increased exponentially. Moving is costly. As a family man, I had a mortgage, two cars with payments, and a new lifestyle, with a stay-at-home wife and two children. Even with a better paying job, there was not enough money to meet our expenses. So, I began working as a server again. Then I began night school majoring in forensic accounting and biblical studies. I had no real family time but knew I had to make more money. On top of everything I was doing, frantic to make more money, I began investing in stocks with the little money I could scrape together. My wife and children hardly saw me at all. I was working sixty-five hours a week and going to school.

My small stock purchases were incredibly successful.

GOD'S FORMULA FOR FINANCIAL FREEDOM

I had remarkable investment success, but here once again I had little return because the investments were so small. Nevertheless, I came to believe I could make a living doing nothing but investing if I only had enough capital to begin with. My investments were so remarkable that they caught the attention of a wealthy trader, and he began to watch what I did more and more closely. He called me throughout the day and wanted to know my trades. He had a lot of money and his returns looked phenomenal to both of us. He did what I did or what I wanted to do. I was happy for the attention which was much like the relationship I had with my father. I mistook our association as friendship. He flattered me and made me financial promises. I failed to recognize his interest in me for what it was. His interest had nothing to do with me as a person. He called me as often as ten times a day, from early morning to late at night, and for a while, I was happy for the attention of a successful man. Eventually, however, I realized that this was not a friendship. He strung me along with promises of compensation and his "tests," to make sure I knew what I was doing. I warned him that if he did not share with me, I would not give him access to my selections. When I cut back and withdrew, our "friendship" ended.

For many reasons, not the least of which was working two jobs, going to night school, and catering to the greed of a new acquaintance, my marriage dissolved. I was devastated and became so depressed and unable to work that I lost my job. But I told myself, *I can invest in stocks*

PROLOGUE

and this time, I will have enough capital with which to buy meaningful amounts of stock. Then I proceeded to use borrowed money, confident that I could not lose, and that's all I could think about.

Quickly, I became caught up in the thrill of making money. I had no income other than borrowed money, and my life became shambles. For a while, my winning streak continued but it was no match for my mounting debt and living expenses. And this is very important: I neglected my devotions. Finally, I acted without giving myself even a few hours of reflection and prayer and, in a moment of panic, I lost on the stock market. Already in credit card debt, the stock market losses were the final straw. I lost more than what I had earned and borrowed. My entire way of life was wiped out in a few days.

It has taken me several years to return to solvency and to incorporate God's Formula into my life. I am now grateful for the recovery and subsequent abundance that God has provided. Now, every day, I make time for God, for my family, and my work.

From my story, I hope you get the sense that you and I are very much alike. For all my early training, I had to learn the hard way. I pray you can be spared the pain of financial failure or even a similar lapse in judgment. I also hope you see in what I have shared the potential for you to move from being broke and penniless, or anywhere in between, into Financial Freedom God's way!

Introduction

This book, *God's Formula for Financial Freedom*, suggests ways for you to change yourself and live a better life, primarily a better life spiritually and financially. For some people, this book will encourage and assure them that they are already on the right path and help them find ways to improve their financial journey. In either case, whether you are just starting out or you are well on your way, it is not easy to change or to "stay the course." But financial security and success are worth the effort. Above all, you deserve the joy that waits for you in the encompassing embrace of God's boundless love. You deserve peace of mind and the ability to care for yourself and your family. As a manager and a pastor, I believe that God promises all of us peace and financial security. I want to put the know-how to get financially fit in your hands.

My own life experiences and the people I meet every day have, in a large part, inspired me to write this book. Just a few weeks ago, when I was shopping in a big box store, I was standing in line waiting for a cashier to check me out. The line was moving very slowly but I refused to use the self-checkout and take jobs from human clerks. So, I waited. And when I finally got to the register, the clerk was elderly. I guessed she was in her eighties. She was working painfully slow, as if every move she made hurt

GOD'S FORMULA FOR FINANCIAL FREEDOM

her. I asked her, "Are you okay?" She answered, "No, it is hard for me to work but my husband just died and without his income, I cannot keep my house. My social security is all I have and it is not enough to pay even the taxes. I will lose my home if I do not work. I wish I didn't have to come out of retirement."

I understood her predicament but all I could give her at the time was my patience and of course, I bagged my own order. She needed a lot more money than I could afford to give her. And a lot more help than just money. I only wish I had met her and her husband earlier in life in order to help them prepare for this moment.

In the same store a little later in the month, I was in line behind a young couple who were using credit cards to buy groceries. They were buying staples, like bread and milk. They maxed out one credit card and pulled out another. It no longer worked. They pulled out a third card and it only worked for a few items. Over half their order was still on the checkout belt. It was clear that they had no money and no more credit cards. They were upset. They had diapers and formula on the checkout line as well. I had enough money with me for what I needed and more, so, at that moment, I bought their order for them. They cried with relief. I felt blessed, fortunate to be able to do that for them. I gave them the phone number of our pastor and I wanted to talk with them some more, but they were embarrassed, and the checkout line was long, so we went our separate ways. I have heard and seen other situations like the ones I

INTRODUCTION

just shared. More people are in more financial trouble than anyone knows.

I myself know what it is like to be destitute even though I was only that far down for a season in my life. I know firsthand that it is a terrible position to be in. Poverty is almost a dirty word these days, and as humiliating as it can be, it should not be embarrassing. There are very limited resources and instruction in school and from parents to teach children about finances. Very few people reach adulthood with all its responsibilities, temptations, and expenses knowing how to handle money. Most of us stumble along with no preparation, no example, no training and we try to imitate the people who seem successful even though quite often, those very people are also in financial difficulty. According to Bankrate.com, "between 55 percent to 63 percent of Americans are ... living paycheck to paycheck.... [And] 72 percent of Americans are not completely financially secure."[1] That is more than one person in two. If you are one of those people or about to become one, this book is for you. If you are sick and tired of living paycheck to paycheck and being in debt, then please, take control of your money. And I ask you sincerely to let God help you to manage your money.

Before we start to talk about what to do with your money, let me be clear, it does not matter how much you have, how much you are paid. You can have a small check or a very big one. Your income may be a trickle of nickels and dimes or a steady stream of thousands of dollars. And still, you can easily find yourself over your head in debt and unable to make ends meet. It does not seem fair, and everyone looks around for someone to blame; it's human nature. On top of this, our embarrassment keeps us quiet. We feel that we cannot talk to our partners or friends about our financial predicament because it's humiliating.

The problem is not a simple one, there's no "bad" guy. It just seems, "the rich get richer, and the poor get poorer." It is a complex cultural phenomenon. And banks and credit card companies like to make money even at the expense of the everyday man's sanity and health. I happen to believe that the enemy wants us broke and in debt as well. It is, after all, easier to tempt us to do bad things when we are desperate. There is massive subtle pressure put on all of us to spend more than we earn and to buy things we do not need. "They" want you to buy a new car, get a loan for new furniture, charge the newest electronics, take a vacation to Bermuda and gamble on our cell phones. The "spend" voice is everywhere. We are promised unbeatable "deals" and big rewards and, of course, satisfaction and fun. And because we anticipate this "fun" we often feel a brief moment of pleasure when we purchase things that are more than what we need or that are more expensive than we can afford. Then that moment of a smile passes, and we are back in the trap of "trying to make ends meet."

Because of technology, what we earn and spend has become increasingly invisible. Our checks go into our accounts by direct deposit and out through paperless billing

INTRODUCTION

and debit cards.

How many of us know how much we actually make? Or how much it costs to live a week or a month? We are a short step away from crypto currency when AI will know every fraction of a cent we earn and spend. Then we will not need to file tax returns, because the big computer in the sky will have a record of every single transaction we make, no matter how big or small. There will be a running record of the taxes we owe. The future of under-the-table work looks bleak. It is important to pay attention to what we earn and spend even though it is simple not to look. Now you may have more credit card debt than you can handle in five years or even in twenty years! If you do not pay attention to your money, someone, many "someone's," will.

I hope I can help you resist all the pressure to spend more than you can afford. I really believe it will take a power greater than me, or you for that matter. I hope more of us will turn to God the Father. Many people address their credit card debt by getting more credit cards. Some apply for loans. In short, we try to get out of the hole by digging it deeper. Financial problems have proved to be at the heart of many illnesses, divorce, and even suicide. The debt problem crept up on us and here we sit, it seems suddenly. What is the solution? Making more money is only half the answer.

As a manager, I received a visit from a man who was making over $600,000 per year. He owned two homes and three high-end cars. He wanted to borrow enough to buy his middle daughter a new car as a graduation gift just as he had done for his eldest. He was looking at a small BMW for her, in the neighborhood of $65,000. His lifestyle seemed impressive, and I am sure his neighbors thought him well-off. I thought so too until I ran his credit check. He had huge mortgages on both homes, all three cars were fully financed and his credit card debt made me wince. There was no way he was going to get a loan from any reputable bank or organization. He had already had to borrow to make payments on some of his existing loans. But to everyone else, he looked successful. I said I could not help him, and he was not surprised. I did ask if he wanted some suggestions as to how to pull back from this catastrophic situation and he listened while I explained some of what I am about to share with you. He acted interested and I hoped he would make the changes.

The more you use God's Formula, the more financially secure you will become. If you have notions about money that are unrealistic or if you have simply never paid attention to how your money comes and goes, following God's formula will help you have realistic expectations and establish good money management habits. If you are new on the path to financial health or if you are well on your way, you will find in Section I, additional power that will amplify your success. I hope what I share here will help you avoid some of the mistakes I made, and if not, help you recuperate more quickly. When you add these habits and

22

INTRODUCTION

practices into your workday and daily life, you will live in God's promises and abundance will follow. Remember, we worship the Blesser, God, not the blessing. Our faith and God's Word promise us we will move beyond having just enough money. I believe that acting in accord with God's scripturally based instructions is essential. For me, it must precede even a durable Money Management Plan. What I believe is not as important to your success as what you believe. I pray that what I share in these pages is in accord with God's *Rhema* Word[1] so that you may hear it clearly and receive it.

For some, the fact that this formula is written from a Christian and scriptural standpoint may be a turnoff. It is possible you are only reading this because someone recommended this book to you. Or you may be a very thorough person who wants to make sure you are doing all you can to succeed financially. No matter what, I hope you can find a way to use God's Formula. It works because it relies on the promises of the living God. And because it is valid, you will find it scientifically and psychologically reliable. You can count on it. When we read, "Wealth gained hastily will dwindle, but whoever gathers little by little will increase it" (Proverbs 13:11, ESV), we respect and care for what we earn. If things come too easily, by swiping a credit card for example, we lose sight of its value. You may have heard, "easy come, easy go."

---

1 It means words spoken to you from God that you have complete understanding in or Scripture for personal application.

GOD'S FORMULA FOR FINANCIAL FREEDOM

Again, "The plans of the diligent lead surely to abundance, but everyone who is hasty comes only to poverty" (Proverbs 21:5, ESV). When you steadily plan what you spend; when you routinely practice earning, you learn the skill and develop the know-how to make and keep money. Over time you will learn how to treat money so that you prosper. You will know how to overcome setbacks and changes in your life. If you think you will always be poor, guess what? You will be. If you see yourself as wealthy only because you have "things," I promise, those things will disappear while true wealth will not. How do you go about changing your attitude toward money to a healthy one? The best way I know is to follow God's direction. Think and behave as God asks. Do this as part of your daily devotion. Rely on God. But if you cannot quite bring yourself to pray, then regularly meditate. Same goes for praise. If you cannot say, "thank You, God," then regularly be grateful; notice the good things in your life. Expect good things. Every day there are good things that happen, and the more you notice them, the more you will see. If you take time to make devotion a routine, you will find it easier to develop good financial habits. In Scripture, God says, "Test Me. See what I will do for you when you do as I ask" (Malachi 3:10, paraphrase).

If you are currently living from paycheck to paycheck; if you have credit card debt or might become homeless if you lose your job, this is your book. If you feel "down" or afraid you will not be able to make ends meet, these pages

INTRODUCTION

are where you need to be. If you are anxious about inflation and how you will buy your groceries, this is indeed your book. If you are tired of seeing the other guy "get ahead" while you fall behind, here is where that ends. You are going to learn to pay attention to your money and use it the way God wants you to.

Before we talk about what to do with your money, let me be clear. You do not need to start rich to get rich. There are a lot of ways to earn money and to spend less. You will not be asked to do without the things you need but you may have to put the brakes on unnecessary spending. The challenge everyone faces is to create a sound financial plan and stick with it. This book suggests ways to honor God, increase your income, eliminate unnecessary purchases, make investments, save money, and live within your means. Many institutions and forces do not want you to keep the money you earn for yourself and your family. Banks, corporations, and even the government want to be in control of your money. I also believe the enemy wants us to be poor, to be broke and in debt. These entities take our money quietly, and some take it relentlessly. The pressure is on for you to buy a new car, get another credit card, buy the newest electronics, take a vacation, gamble on your cell phone ... the list goes on. You are told you can own "the American dream." And while it is very good to live in the USA, nobody can own a dream.

On top of this cunning and powerful pressure to spend, to borrow, there is no basic course, no training in how to manage money. For the most part, your parents were probably untrained as well. So, it looks like it's normal to borrow and to buy things on credit and to carry unpaid balances. We go out to eat and charge the meal on a credit card. Why do we eat out so much to begin with? We borrow tens of thousands to go to college. Why has it become "normal" to get a huge student loan? Are there other ways to go to college? Is college so "right" for everyone and is it always what we should do just out of high school? Since when is it "normal" for people to go into bankruptcy again and again? Why do people lose their homes? Why are people in their forties and beyond still paying for student loans?

There are legitimate ways to earn enough to live on and ways to curb spending that allow you to save and still have a good life. When you pay attention to your money and handle it in sensible ways, ways that God endorses, you will start to have sufficient money and a fulfilling life. How do you go about changing your attitude toward money to a healthy one? The best way I know is to follow God's direction. Think and behave as God asks. Do this as part of your daily devotion. Rely on God. Receive His help and support, His blessings.

After Section I, when you move into Section II of this book, you will find financial suggestions that can help you stay out of debt, earn enough to live on, save, and invest. Section II is by itself a good, sound outline for successful money management. Each topic that is touched on there

INTRODUCTION

has been the focus of hundreds of books, hours of Internet presentations, and semesters of college courses. Once you employ the formula for Financial Freedom, you can build on it, make it stronger. What you have in your hands is enough to get you started in recovery and growth. Your Financial Freedom will grow most quickly and securely—I believe you will prosper—when you knit the Spiritual Foundation of Section I and the Financial Structure of Section II together. I am eager to see you enjoying the blessings of Financial Freedom.

Part One: Spiritual Foundation

CHAPTER 1:

A Day with God

MY SCHEDULE OR MY EFFORT TO "PRAY WITHOUT CEASING"

I offer you a sample of how I spend my day and hope it will help you realize—make real—God's Formula for Financial Freedom in your life.

(My days are like anyone else's. I acknowledge God's loving presence throughout the day)

BETWEEN 5–5:30 A.M., I WAKE UP AND PRAISE GOD

My praise is something like this: "Thank You, Father God, for my refreshing sleep and for waking me to this day full of promise and potential.

With You, I know this day will be successful.

GOD'S FORMULA FOR FINANCIAL FREEDOM

Thanks to You, I know I will recognize opportunity and I will act on it to the best of my ability.

With Your help, I know I will be productive.

Thank You for shining out; help me to show up.

Amen."

I invite God's direction, wait a second, and then write down some actual intentions for the day.

I thank God for the confidence to perform in a meaningful way.

(At about 6 a.m., I lie down for a few more minutes)

AROUND 7–7:30 A.M.

I have a light breakfast, usually cereal, maybe some fruit

I physically and spiritually nourish myself.

I read a little from Proverbs

Shower (and often sing)

Before I leave the house, I pack my lunch

(I usually plan my supper so that I will have leftovers for lunch)

As I drive to work, I pray out loud and often my prayers are for the well-being of people who have asked me to pray for them or for the people God has put in my heart. I pray for trouble spots I may have heard of on the news or in the paper.

AT WORK AROUND 8:45 A.M.

I pray as I meet my co-workers and clients. Just a short prayer, quietly to myself:

"Thank You, God, for allowing me to be of service to ... (and I name the person)."

As I tackle projects, answer the phone, read regulations, and directives, I say a brief heartbeat of a prayer:

"Let me do this the way You want me to do it."

Or Just:

"Thy Will be Done."

As I move through my day, I ask God to help my efforts to add to the success of my workplace and the well-being of the people I meet.

I often ask for God's help in managing specific projects or undertakings.

ABOUT 12:30–1 P.M. LUNCH

Again, I eat and read Scripture, usually from a 365/day Bible plan, an app on my phone

AROUND 4:30–5 P.M.

On the way home, I reflect on my day and thank God for all His blessings.

Often, I fix my own supper, but again, there will be leftovers for lunch

At my supper meal, I read Psalms.

There is time with my family, and I give them my full presence and attention.

Sometimes I read, watch shows, or attend Christian functions. I tie up some personal financial odds and ends.

ABOUT 10 P.M.

I close my day with praise

I may say something like, "Thank You, Father God, for leading me through this day. Thank You for helping me make good decisions. Thank You for the ideas and thoughts that seemed especially to be inspired by You. Thank You for all the blessings that will come from the work we did today. Thank You for nurturing ____(and I fill in the blank with the current private, spiritual, or business initiative/seed). Amen."

I was surprised at the time it took to write this down because the prayers and devotions seem to take so little actual time. I mention this because if you decide to do something similar,

A DAY WITH GOD

it will not interfere with your day; it will cost you nothing. In fact, your day will be brighter, better.

CHAPTER 2:

Give to God

While I vigorously pursue and practice sound financial knowledge and investments, I first and foremost do everything the way God wants me to financially. My devotion to God comes before anything else and within that framework, I strive to be the best financial manager I can be.

One of the things that led to this book, *God's Formula for Financial Freedom*, began when I started research and study on finances mentioned in the Bible. While doing this, I found that the Bible talks much about finances. Finances is the second biggest topic in the Bible after love; it's spoken about more than hell and salvation. To me this was a staggering discovery. I believe the reason for this being the second biggest topic is because our physical health, relationships, and emotional well-being are attached to our finances. When we have financial difficulties, the likelihood of divorce increases, the risks of heart attacks and strokes increase and rates of depression rise. According to the

University of Nottingham in the UK, "people who struggle with debt are more than twice as likely to suffer from depression."[2] The most important reason for the writing of this book is that my personal life was totally upside down. I was bankrupt in every area of my life. I was at a point of desperation knowing that I needed to hand over this area of my life to God, because I had not been doing what I knew God's Word said I should be doing.

After I started putting this formula into practice, my financial life improved dramatically! So much, that my pastor asked me to share what I was doing regarding tithing. I started giving 20 percent of my gross income: 10 percent as a tithe and 10 percent as a seed. Then I began to give more, to seed, as my finances grew. In these recent years, my gross income includes my salary and side hustles, my dividends, and profits from investments. Because I am financially doing well, my tithing apparently stands out as significant. Currently I am giving a 10 percent tithe and seeding 25 percent. That is 35 percent of my income that goes to the ministry. That is part of my spiritual development, because while I have grown spiritually, I have also grown and continue to grow financially. I truly look forward to the day of giving 90 percent to God and living on 10 percent. In my discussion with my pastor, I re-told my story of recovery and how I had woven my faith in Christ into my daily and financial life. He suggested I share this information with members of the congregation. I pulled together a Zoom presentation that allowed for several weeks of presentations. We allowed for give and take, a song of praise and a prayer. That process occurred about six years ago and was followed by a second set of recorded Zoom broadcasts. When I realized how in demand this information was, I decided to draw it together in a book. That is where we are now.

I am so grateful that I decided to tithe. It was not easy at first because when I began, I had just filed for bankruptcy. The word *tithe* in Hebrew means a tenth, and a handful of both Christians and Jews take Leviticus 27:30 literally and tithe one-tenth of their gross income. Some sects require tithing as a condition of membership, but they are not a large portion of the religious community. To say it differently, even people who have Scripture that talks about tithing, do not tithe. Christians look to the New Testament and to 2 Corinthians 9:7 which says, "Each of you must give as you have made up your mind, not reluctantly or under compulsion, for God loves a cheerful giver" (NRSVA). As I studied the Bible, I found that there is a lot more encouragement to give the tithe to God and having 10 percent be the starting point in your giving journey.

For me, when I prayed about tithing, I knew it was right and that I needed to act in accord with God's original instruction. God is, for me, the origin of all things. It seems widely acknowledged that if we want to grow spiritually, we must act in spiritual ways. For me, I wonder if as Christians, we may have forgotten that God works spiritually, mentally, physically, and financially. Christ turned water to wine. The multitude was fed with a "lunch basket" of loaves and fishes ... and there were bushels of leftovers! God fed the Israelites with manna and sent them flocks of quail to eat. He did this daily for forty years. Joseph prepared the country of Egypt for a famine of seven years at God's direction. And throughout the Bible, the Torah, and other Scriptures as well, God has demonstrated the power to not only make, but to shape, the world we live in. God's Spirit is in all things, including the physical and the financial. The Bible is full of instructions on how we may prosper. It's important for me that I follow God's Word, in all things. If I want to grow spiritually, I need to worship with all my surrendered self. With practice, I am strengthened by that worship. And if I want to experience God's works in the physical world, I need to worship as I am instructed; to give to His creation. I need to support His intention, His way of life, for this world and the next. And that means I give what matters in all things and that includes financially.

In the Bible, next to the topic of love, the most talked about topic is that of prosperity or abundance. God wants us to enjoy His *entire* creation! And He wants us to support His work and will reward us for that support. There are many verses that tell us how we are to grow financially. It suddenly clicked in my mind that if I want to grow in abundance, I must worship God with physical things that support both His kingdom and His people in all things.

To worship fully, I must tithe AND build into my life the

behaviors and devotions that I am instructed to cultivate. Even when I had no credit, and was in bankruptcy, I began to give all that I could to God as part of my routine devotional practice. In those early days when I first started tithing, there were times when I was not able to pay my bills. Because I knew that, we are promised abundance in God's Word, and while I was doing significantly better than when I first started, I was still working two jobs and trusting God to meet my needs. I started to seed, and my income improved. I seeded more and I brought alms and first fruits into my giving. God's formula for Financial Freedom was shaping up in my life.

When that happened, God supernaturally made a way to meet my needs, and I had money left over! I received promotions, had financial dreams that led to making wise investments, experienced windfalls, and found smarter ways to economize. Much of it was unexpected; it felt like I was given "gifts." When that first year of tithing and seeding was done, I had more than I ever had before.

One of the people who attended my early presentations of *God's Formula for Financial Freedom* on Zoom, once asked me if she was right in teaching her son how to handle credit cards at the age of eighteen. And of course, I said yes. But if I had to answer that question today, I would suggest before anyone is taught about credit cards, they should be taught about how to give to God and how to give to others. Children can learn to give to God. Figuring and adjusting what you give to God's work is at least a monthly endeavor. Depending on whether your income comes in slowly or quickly, it requires record keeping with an "eyes on" approach. Tracking your income, looking for ways to protect and increase it, is a good practice to get into. And, yes, knowing how to manage credit cards is a valuable skill, but the most important skill is to acknowledge God financially, knowing how to manage your money and not live in the bondage of debt. When a person tracks their income in order to know how much to tithe, they also pay attention to their money. You develop, grow, and cultivate what you pay attention to.

I kept track of my income and seeded a bit more, until I edged all the way up to 35 percent. What happened then is perhaps coincidental, but I like to believe it is fulfillment of God's promise. I found I was being blessed to the point of overflow and found I didn't need credit cards anymore—this was amazing!

Let me give you a word of caution, if you are in a partnership and you contribute to the household expenses, please remember to discuss tithing with your partner. If possible, make sure your prospective partner wants to tithe as well. And remember especially when you first begin to tithe, you may not be able to purchase as much or the same quality of things you did as before you tithed. This change will affect you and your partner and children if you have them. If possible, it is important to move into tithing together. Especially in the beginning, there needs to be discussions about how much to tithe, save, spend.

GIVE TO GOD

For me, tithing certainly comes before investing. If things were ideal, the discussion about tithing and seeding would come before marriage. It's not going to be easy, and you will have moments of doubt and fears of failure, but if you remind yourself of God's promises found in His Word, you will be able to overcome these moments.

CHAPTER 3:

Alms and Firstfruits

When researching the four types of giving found in the Bible, I asked the Lord what a good starting place in a Financial Freedom journey would be. What the Lord led me to, which may be controversial, is that a place to start can be alms and first fruits. The reason I start with alms and first fruits is because this is a one-time giving, whereas tithing and seeding is consistent. I believe that many believers have a hard time tithing and seeding due to financial mistakes they have made in their lives. By starting with alms and first fruits, this is an obtainable goal to meet. By starting off with small successes and working your way up, this will excite and encourage you to keep going; starting with one small step of faith will lead you to taking a leap of faith.

When you start giving first fruits, you will see salary increases, bonuses, and promotions; these "first fruits" are often unexpected and amazing. The reason behind our first fruits giving is to show God that we are not in love with money, and we acknowledge Him for the increase. You are not prospering because you love money but because you love God. If you want to know more about first fruits, there are thirty-one verses in the Bible that speak on first fruits.

An applicable verse from the Old Testament is Proverbs 3:9–10 (ESV):

> *"Honor the LORD with your wealth and with the first fruits of all your produce [income]; then your barns will be filled with plenty, and your vats will be bursting with wine."*

We are asked to worship the Lord God with our wealth.

Then from Romans 11:16 (ESV):

> *"If the dough offered as firstfruits is holy, so is the whole lump, and if the root is holy, so are the branches."*

Certainly, this verse applies to people who are not Israelites, being sanctified through Jesus. But it also, as does so much of the Bible, tells us to acknowledge and be grateful for each new beginning, or first fruit, and to acknowledge the gift as one that will continue to grow, to produce abundantly.

And finally, we are instructed to give alms. The reason for this is charity. This will sometimes be a spontaneous gift. We may pay for someone's groceries in a checkout line when we see they need help. We can donate to a food

ALMS AND FIRSTFRUITS

bank! Stay awake to opportunities to help. As you practice these four important scriptural instructions, these four ways of giving, or formula, you will find you have the money to be generous. Enjoy and be thankful for having enough money. Helping others can, of itself, be rewarding. Be on the lookout for opportunities to give. Or we may pick one or more charities, like the Red Cross, or say the American Juvenile Diabetes Foundation. I also like the Salvation Army, but you choose the charity you like! I research the background of any charities to which I give to ensure they use as much donated money as possible for their intended purpose. I am personally turned off when I learn that executives in a charitable organization are drawing preposterously large salaries. Matthew 6:1–4 essentially says that when you give alms to the needy or poor, do it out of sincere devotion to God. Do not give to be "seen" by others, to be perceived as a generous man or woman. Be as God wants you to be—quite simply, a generous person.

In Proverbs 19:17 (ESV) we hear, "*Whoever is generous to the poor lends to the LORD, and he will repay him for his deed.*" Charity, acts of kindness, be they monetary or not, will be repaid to those who act out of love for God and their fellowman.

CHAPTER 4:

Above All, Tithe

When we serve God, we want to give back a tenth of what He originally gave us because we do this out of obedience and love for God. By doing what He asks, we learn to trust in God's care and guidance. After you begin to tithe, pay attention, God will meet your needs and recession and depression will bypass you; it rebukes the devil (Malachi 3:10–11; 2 Corinthians 9:8). God will show up and show out in ways that you never thought would happen or could imagine. Tithing has not received the attention it deserves. I believe it should be an integral part of worship. As I tithe, my faith, my confidence in God, has grown.

We are asked to tithe 10 percent of our gross, total income to God, every week or whenever we get paid. We use whichever time frame allows us to make the best determination of what we need to tithe on. If we have a single steady paycheck, paying a 10 percent tithe once a month can make sense. But if we also have a side hustle, rental properties, or commission-based income, then our

GOD'S FORMULA FOR FINANCIAL FREEDOM

income varies from week to week and so will the 10 percent.

Your tithe is always given to the church you attend and only that church. That is right. Tithe to the actual church or place of worship that you attend. Keep the lights on where your friends, where your congregation, gather. Keep the heat and air conditioning working where you get together. Make that place comfortable, attractive, inviting. Then, it is even more likely that your "church" will grow. People will want to join gatherings where it is comfortable, where everything works as it should and the environment and proceedings are uplifting. You are much more likely to know what good works your place of worship is doing when you attend that site and see firsthand! You will get to know the people you worship with and they you. It's better when the speakers and microphones work and everyone can hear what the pastor is saying. When you support the church you attend, you will reap the benefit of seeing your tithe pay off. It is a bit simplistic to say but it is so true. We care more about what we "spend" our money on than what we get for free. And when you come to see how God returns your gift, you will also become increasingly able to recognize "right" returns that are truly a blessing.

If God lays it on your heart, you may ask your church to use some of the money you give in a specific way. But typically, your tithe is used at your church's discretion. You may be led to want to attend or participate in your church's business meetings. If you do, this will improve your understanding of not only what your church is doing for others but also your personal ability to allocate your own money appropriately. You will see and better understand how difficult, yet, important it is to budget within your resources.

Once you have begun tithing, then you can also enjoy the blessings of seeding, first fruits, and almsgiving. God will help you decide how much to seed or how much and when to give alms. Apply the "formula" of giving in unison among all four. By the way, first fruits are an occasional gift which is triggered by a onetime event, like a pay-raise or a windfall. Seeding on the other hand, will be the way of giving that moves you from a comfortable lifestyle into abundance. Keep reminding yourself that giving in these well-defined ways is NOT about giving to God so that He will give to you. Rather, when we give obediently or from compassion, we reap the benefits of obedience and compassion. And because God is beyond limits, you will also be rewarded by His standard and that is abundance.

As servers or servants, we give to God, His church, and His people as instructed. As we have discussed, tithing is at the core of the formula. I think my tithe caught the eye of my pastor because it went up significantly as I made more money. We are asked to tithe in both the Old and the New Testaments. Our motive for giving is, yes, obedience. We do what God wants rather than what our egos want. We give as directed, in confident faith, that our Lord God will care for us. As we come to appreciate how much God loves us, our self-esteem, our healthy self-love, and confidence will

GOD'S FORMULA FOR FINANCIAL FREEDOM

also improve. That 10 percent of our gross income will not deprive us. Do not let fear of want deter you. Your routine tithe of 10 percent will result in significant, multilevel blessings.

In Malachi 3:10 (ESV) we are told:

> *"Bring the full tithe into the storehouse, that there may be food in my house. And thereby put me to the test, says the LORD of hosts, if I will not open the windows of heaven for you and pour down for you a blessing until there is no more need."*

Then again in 2 Corinthians 9:8 (ESV):

> *"God is [perfectly] able to make all grace abound to you, so that having all sufficiency in all things at all times, you may abound in every good work."*

CHAPTER 5:

Seeding and Using Talents

After you begin tithing, and you want to stretch your faith even further, sow seeds. Seeding simply means that you give over and above the 10 percent tithe to the church or ministry that God leads. How much? It depends on what you feel God leads you to give. Even 1 percent more is better than nothing, but can you do 5 percent? How much are you willing to stretch your faith? When we put our focus and attention on seeding, the harvest will lead us to a place of total debt cancellation. Our motivation when we seed stems from our faith and confidence that God will reward our seeding, that will result in a return of thirty, sixty or even 100 times over (Matthew 13:23). Everyone wants 100 times over from their seed, but are you willing to go through the 100 times test? In other words, everyone wants the glory, but no one wants to live the story.

For me there are several Bible verses that reinforce

GOD'S FORMULA FOR FINANCIAL FREEDOM

God's intention to reward us, to multiply our appropriate use of giving, all to God's greater glory. To begin with, we have Matthew 25:29 (ESV): *"For to everyone who has will more be given, and he will have an abundance. But from the one who has not, even what he has will be taken away."*

Next when you read chapter 25 in Matthew, you see the word *talent.* In this parable, the master entrusted each of three servants with different amounts of talents. In that time, one talent was the equivalent of nearly twenty year's salary. Just receiving one talent could allow a person to retire. So, each servant had been given a lot of money, even the man who received only one talent had been entrusted with a significant amount of money. The first two wisely invested and used the talents entrusted to their care to earn even more. They added it to their master's account. The third man hid his one talent, buried it, and while he bragged about how he kept it "safe," the master scolded him for not using what He gave him and then fired him. The point here can be simple or as open to interpretation as any other parable. We can interpret this parable to mean that God wants us to use what He gives us; whatever that may be, be it money, a pretty voice, intellect … whatever. In God's formula, I like to emphasize the original meaning. If God gives us "money," use it to help His kingdom prosper! And then He will help us prosper even more, and together you and God's kingdom will prosper abundantly! The enemy subtracts, divides, and reduces what we value, especially if we live in doubt and fear. God, Jehovah-Jireh, opens the

SEEDING AND USING TALENTS

way to prosperity; He multiplies our gifts.

Over and above tithing, we "seed." The concept of seeding from our income comes from the parable about sowing seeds in Matthew 13:3–9 and Luke 8:4–8. I find it interesting that this lesson is told twice, in two separate places in the New Testament. In these parables, we are instructed to sow seeds in fertile ground, ground where it may be expected to grow, to multiply. Ground that is not too dry or rocky. Ground that is not choked with weeds. We are expected to tend this seed, to water it, to "pray" over it. And we "feed" our seed with praise; we thank God for the prosperity of our church's endeavors and initiatives, the seed. The tender plants that grow from those seeds thrive with praise. Left untended, dropped on the ground, forgotten, the seed and young plants will dry up or be choked with weeds of worry and doubt. Weeds and arid times of doubt, of fear, of worry, will stifle success and growth. If we want what we have planted to grow and thrive, we must act in confidence. We must tend to what we have started daily with prayer and praise. And as we pray and acknowledge God as the source of all goodness and abundance; as we praise God for His loving-kindness and the blessing of prosperity, doubt and fear are driven out of our heads and hearts, and we can move forward in increasing confidence and rational thought.

Our "seeds," like our tithes, should be given to churches and/or ministries that help spread the Word of God. You seed as you are led to give. It can certainly be more than

GOD'S FORMULA FOR FINANCIAL FREEDOM

1 or 2 percent. When you begin to live in ever increasing abundance, to have enough money and then even more, it can be easier to give to God what is already His. A gift of 10 percent tithe and 10 percent seed can be a doable amount even though it will be 20 percent of your gross income. Tithing 10 percent and seeding as well may feel like a stretch when you first begin. But it will soon be clear that you have more than sufficient, that you have abundant spiritual and financial resources from which to draw.

Keep in mind the nature of seeds. When they are first planted, they are under the soil; for a few days, maybe a week or more, we do not see them grow. But they do. Seeds, when properly planted, *do* grow, even when we cannot see them. Know this and thank God. While what we plant is in God's hands, the infant seed begins to grow unseen. Be aware that God is working to make what we planted grow. It is symbolic of all growth, both seen and unseen. It may help us to walk in faith more boldly to make a vision board, to imagine what may come to be. Or we may talk among our friends and imagine together some things that may happen when the seeds we have planted grow to maturity. We must water, feed, and weed what is planted. We cultivate the seed through praise and worship and praying over our seed. We can anticipate and be happy that our seeds will result in a harvest, and we should give thanks before and as they mature. It can't hurt to be reminded that different shapes and sizes of plants and fruits will grow from seeds that look pretty much alike when they are first planted. Thank God

SEEDING AND USING TALENTS

in advance, praise Him for what is to come. "The depth of your praise will determine the magnitude of your harvest."[3] Be confident in God. Through our faith, not only will what we plant be multiplied but so will we. I see this promise in Deuteronomy 1:11 (ESV): "May the LORD, the God of your fathers, make you a thousand times as many as you are and bless you, as he has promised." And in John 10:10 (ESV), Christ says, "The thief comes only to steal and kill and destroy. I came that they may have life and have it abundantly."

When I first gave at the 20 percent level, I began to see a harvest shortly thereafter. Again, I wish I had started giving at this level sooner. My tithe and my seeding are now 35 percent of my gross income, and I am happy to say that even though I give more to the church, because of God's blessing, I still have even more money than I have ever had.

Tithing and seeding can occur together. First, we tithe, and our tithe rises to the 10 percent level as quickly as we can. Next, we begin to seed. The more we seed, the more abundant the expected "harvest." As we do what we are led by the Holy Spirit to do—as part of our work of obedience and devotion—the return will grow beyond our expectations. Make sure you reflect and pray until you are at peace with what you can give. I once tithed and seeded my entire paycheck. This was a stretch of my faith having to totally rely on God to meet my needs and to believe that He could! Let me tell you, He surely did and then some!

There have been a few times in my financial faith journey that God has told me to give Him everything and even bless someone with my car. This wasn't easy and took a massive amount of faith, but each time, it got a little bit easier.

But be warned. The enemy, Satan, will try to sow seeds of doubt and worry in your mind through others and your own concerns. You may be plagued with doubts, worry, and fear—these are considered "weeds" that we read of in the parables. Even though we have carefully chosen our church, one that is closely tied to the will of God, we may still have fear. Through doubt, worry, and fear, it will cause a delay in our harvest because we are constantly digging up our seed to see where we are in our harvest. Satan's goal is to cause us to abandon our seed, but if we are consistently watering our seed through meditating on the Word of God and His promises and praising Him "feeding your seed," then your seed will grow and your harvest will be plenty! I, too, praise God for the harvest that made it possible for me to seed to begin with. Praise increases confidence and keeps us attentive. Thank God for the harvest that will grow from our immature seeds. Thank God for His goodness and many blessings, spiritual, physical, and financial. Praise God for what you have right now and for what is on the way! Thank God for the anticipated harvest!

Yes, your first tithing, your first seeds may feel awkward. But we learned quickly to charge things we cannot afford. We made room for credit card debt. Our charge cards promise nothing but immediate self-gratification and at

SEEDING AND USING TALENTS

best a good credit rating, but millions of Americans give their unearned money away. If you are walking in faith, devoted to God, your tithe and seeds will produce a tangible harvest. When you tithe and seed to God's kingdom, you will reap abundance. When you practice tithing, you will be blessed; you will profit in ways that often defy imagination. When you charge, you often get things you do not need and frequently incur debt. The money can come out of your pocket for either tithing or consuming. The choice, for me, seems easy.

Stay focused on what you have planted; pay attention to your garden. Like any other garden, if we do not watch and tend to the new seeds and tender sprouts, small weeds will appear in a few days. Weeds can grow quickly and choke the young plants. Pray for discernment, for inspiration, for the knowledge to determine what in your garden needs to stay, what needs to go. It is important, especially when the plants and weeds are first coming in to pull the weeds while they are still small. There are even times when the new plants are too close to each other, and they need to be spread out or culled. If we lapse into inattentiveness, the weeds can tangle in with the good plants and make it harder to pull the weeds without disrupting the young plants. Do not brood and worry when the "seeds" are freshly planted. In these early weeks, we may be plagued or beset with unexpected expenses or setbacks. I believe these things are works of the enemy. Rebuke these trials. See the obstacles as only temporary. Be confident that there will be seasons of planting and reaping, just as promised in Genesis 8:22 (ESV), "While the earth remains, seedtime and harvest, cold and heat, summer and winter, day and night, shall not cease."

Wait attentively and patiently for the harvest, and while waiting, listen to music that inspires. Attend meetings of Christian fellowship. Search for ways to cultivate your own growth in the light of God's love. Read your Bible. Explore healthy investment methodologies. Talk and plan with good people. Text a friend some of your good news. Invite the Holy Spirit into your day-to-day work. Play with your kids. Garden. Take your dog for a walk; pet the cat. Above all, pray and praise God. BE the cheerful giver!

When we praise God and rejoice in His goodness and boundless generosity, then what we have planted, our church's endeavors, will prosper and grow, as will our confidence. You will be present to see it. You will experience it. Continue to pray. Prayer is like water to your seed. Praise God, and praise will strengthen the seeds and help them mature into a bountiful harvest. We are not looking for pretense or the posturing of the greedy or arrogant; we expect the abundant, meaningful blessings of God in our lives and in the world. Speak your confident prayer and praise aloud whenever you can.

"God, thank You for these healthy seeds and this nourishing soil in which to sow them. I put my confidence in the law of seedtime and harvest, and I know that You

SEEDING AND USING TALENTS

are working on our behalf to bring this planting to fruition. Thank You for letting me see your bountiful work in my life and in my community. Amen."

Anchor yourself with statements of faith; use your own wording; describe the initiative that you have seeded. Expect great results and God's favor. Know that, when you "sow" financially, you will reap financially.

While I pray that people may find Jesus as Savior, I think God also answers prayers that ask for a closer walk in His light and love. I pray for specific seeds; I name them. One such "seed" is this book, *God's Formula for Financial Freedom.* I pray "that this information, here in your hands will help you to a solvent and abundant life. I pray that you will put this material to work in your life and that as a result, your finances will improve dramatically and that you will find the confidence to use more and more of this formula. I pray that you experience for yourself the fulfillment of God's love and prosperity. Amen."

As I go forward, I take from Genesis 1:11 the belief that all that is planted, all that grows, will produce according to its "kind." That orange seeds will produce orange trees; if I want friends, I must be friendly. If you want to be blessed financially, you must give financially. The list goes on and on. I need help; I must be helpful. I need better health. I must do healthier things, take better care of myself, and so on.

GOD'S FORMULA FOR FINANCIAL FREEDOM

Say your prayers, in your own words. Water your seed. If you like, use the prayers I offer as templates, as examples.

"God, I have sown my financial seeds, and I am expecting them to produce after their own kind in the form of financial blessing, as a financial harvest." Pray aloud. Speak these prayers and ones like them every day, throughout the day.

There may be unexpected delays or setbacks but you will prosper. I am tempted to tell you about my own specific successes as the result of this formula, but I hesitate because they are so miraculous as to perhaps seem unbelievable. I am tithing and seeding at about 35 percent as of this writing and my budget allows for saving, investing, and a life where I can be generous and comfortable. I have had unexpected promotions, dreams that revealed specific investment opportunities, bonuses, windfalls, the list goes on. Above all, my faith, my relationship with God, have grown stronger. My faith has also been rewarded, as will yours. When you use this formula, share your successes with others. As you share, these will be words of encouragement to others to help them grow in their financial journey.

Tithing, seeding, first fruits, and almsgiving, done together, are the Formula for Financial Freedom. And we must use all four ways of giving. When we look at our financial structure, there are many ways to save, many ways to earn, and we may pick and choose from among them. But to make the formula work, we must give it in all four ways.

SEEDING AND USING TALENTS

As you give, the quality of both your day-to-day and your spiritual life will grow and improve. You will find that you provide a good life for your family. With God's help, you will make wise, carefully considered financial decisions. You and your household will grow financially secure. I believe that as you continue to follow this formula, you can secure generational wealth and live your life in accord with the will of God.

CHAPTER 6:

Bible Verses become Statements of Faith

As I read the Bible, certain verses, sections, even chapters make a more significant impact. When this occurs, I often make that verse into a prayer or a statement of faith, sometimes both. This practice etches the verse more deeply in my heart, makes it "breathe," as I move through my day. When I say verses in my own voice, they seem more personal and my relationship with God more intimate. This experience strengthens me, and I believe it can also strengthen you. So here are a few examples of what I do. Please, be encouraged to use your own words, make your prayers, your praise, your faith—your worship—your personal conduit between you and God Almighty. These verses are how you water your seed.

Mark 4:26–27 (NRSVA), *"The kingdom of God is as if someone would scatter seed on the ground, and would sleep and rise night and day, and the seed would sprout and grow, he does not know how."*

PRAYER/PRAISE:

"Thank You, God, for causing our initiatives to thrive. Thank You for making the office where I work more productive and the people who work here more content. Thank You for the number of loans we have been able to give and for the quality of service we have provided. Thank You for all the positive feedback we have had from customers."

Or you might say,

"Thank You, God, for helping our young people's Sunday school class to grow. These past six months, four more children joined our class. Thank You that their parents came with them and that they trust us to care for them while they attend a class tailored for adults."

Another version: "Thank You, Lord, for giving me such healthy ideas and for finding ways to nurture and develop these plans. Thank You for helping me to see ways to invest and buy property. I am especially grateful that these initiatives will help both the buyer and the seller."

And another verse: Job 36:11 (ESV), *"If they listen and serve him, they complete their days in prosperity, and their years in pleasantness [contentment]."*

We might pray, "God, I am happy to obey You! Because I obey You, my faith grows and You surround me with

BIBLE VERSES BECOME STATEMENTS OF FAITH

prosperity and pleasantness. Thank You for Your blessings. I am content and comfortable because of all You provide."

This prayer dispels doubt and strengthens your faith.

Psalm 115:12–14 (NLT), "The LORD remembers us and will bless us.... He will bless those who fear the LORD.... May the LORD richly bless both you and your children."

"Thank You, God, for watching over me and what I do. Thank You for protecting my family and increasing our financial security. Thank You for the good food, home, and education that You provided my loved ones. Amen."

Speak aloud when you can so that you may hear your own voice giving praise. Pray aloud when you have a private moment. Be confident that God sees and hears you. Hearing the prayer, even your own prayer will be uplifting, and you will find increased ability to move on to more and bigger things. Your expectations will grow, as will your ability to perform.

One of my favorites is, *"Give, and you will receive. Your gift will return to you in full—pressed down, shaken together to make room for more, running over, and poured into your lap. The amount you give will determine the amount you get back"* (Luke 6:38, NLT).

Create your own prayer or statement of faith from this verse. You might say, "Thank You, God, for giving me so much. Even though You said You would give me more than I gave You, I am touched by Your generosity! It is so much more than I expected! My faith is strengthened by Your gifts."

> *2 Corinthians 9:6 (ESV), "Whoever sows sparingly will also reap sparingly, and whoever sows bountifully will also reap bountifully."*

You might say, "Thank You, Holy Lord, for allowing me to financially support so many initiatives through my church and privately. Thank You for giving me the strength to step out in faith and financially plant these seeds. Let the good these initiatives will do be a blessing to my family, my church, and my community."

Or "Thank You, Father, for moving me into this bountiful new life! Thank You for giving me everything I need and even more! Help me to use the blessings You give me in ways that glorify You! May other people see Your goodness and greatness and be moved to obey You. Amen."

Not too long ago, I prayed, "Father God, we thank You for everything You are doing for us. Help us to hear Your *Rhema** Word. Help us to understand Your direction and use it in our daily lives. Thank You for all You continue to do and for all You teach us about love. Thank You for teaching us how to water and nurture our seeds, our initiatives, and endeavors."

BIBLE VERSES BECOME STATEMENTS OF FAITH

*Rhema God's specific word to you at a specific time for a specific purpose.

At the moment, I am particularly enjoying John 15:7–8 and John 15:15–16, (ESV):

"If you abide in me, and my words abide in you, ask whatever you wish, and it will be done for you. By this my Father is glorified, that you bear much fruit and so prove to be my disciples…. I have called you friends, for all that I have heard from my Father I have made known to you…. whatever you ask the Father in my name, he may give it to you."

"Thank You, God, that the readers of this book have come this far and can now pray prayers that are written for them or that they write themselves. These new friends have the information they need to let You lead them and guide them into prosperity and abundance. And the glory of all this Financial Freedom, precious Lord, will be Yours. Amen."

May God smile on you and give you peace. Amen

Part Two:
Financial Structure

CHAPTER 7:

Meet the Financial You

If all you can hear is your own ego and your own thoughts, you may have never had much faith in anything outside yourself or never met the part of yourself that can take care of money. I had to learn to rely on God, and tithing and giving really helped me do that. I also had to learn to manage money. I know you can do both. We have spent a lot of time suggesting that you put faith in God. Right here and now let us also get to know that you, with God's help, can manage what it costs for you to live. You can learn to manage your income and your expenses. When you become conscientious in how you use money, when you stop worrying and fantasizing, you begin to grow into a financially responsible person. When you acknowledge God with your financial gifts, you see money for what it is, not what you may imagine it to be.

Usually, it is easiest to add up your income rather than

GOD'S FORMULA FOR FINANCIAL FREEDOM

your expenses, especially if you have one job with a single paycheck. If that is the case, look at your pay stub. If you are a couple and you both work, you have two sources of income. Each of you tithes on their own gross income. How much do you make before any deductions are taken from your pay? That is your gross income. If you make $4,000 a week before taxes, you make a gross salary of $208,000 a year (52 x $4,000 = $208,000). That is easy. But if your income varies during the year or even the month, if for example you are a real estate broker or an entrepreneur, your gross pay can vary widely from month to month. Then you must figure your income on average. If you make $10,000 in January, $4,000 in February, $7,000 in March, and $4,500 in April and May, your average for those five months is $30,000/5 or $6,000 per month. That is your average gross income for a month. When your income varies from month to month, use an average of twelve months if you can, or even consider using the lowest amount you made to be conservative. Remember that taxes will be due before or at least by April 15. Recalculate your income at the end of each month as your finances grow. You will gradually, with God's help, become a more skillful earner. You are going to recognize opportunities for growth and increased earnings. You're going to find ways to keep earnings and, with God's help, you will improve. This is simple but let it sink in because you will want to stay aware of your income to get to a place where you can not only tithe what is appropriate but also pay your bills, save, and invest. Stay aware of the money you earn, be ready to discover ways to make more.

MEET THE FINANCIAL YOU

For this exercise, you need to figure your net income, which is your actual take-home pay after taxes, tithes, and other deductions. While your gross pay might be $4,000, your net income per week could easily be $3,500 and if that is what you earn a week, then that is what you can spend and how much you can allocate. You need to figure your financial plan on what is often called your take-home pay. Next, you want to figure out how much it costs you to live. This is a little harder because you may not have a single place where all your expenses are listed. Fill in the actual amount wherever you have expenses.

What are the monthly costs for each line item? You can get help pulling the figures together by gathering any of your credit card or bank statements. If you use several cards, then gather statements from them all. Go back three or more months. If you make cash purchases, try to recapture that as well. Did you borrow money from anyone? Your fixed expenses stay fairly stable but in order to capture variable expenses, you may need to estimate. I always recommend going a little on the high side on estimates. Beside each category, put your actual or best estimated cost per month. Then add all the figures in your list together. Now you have a grand total of what, on average, you spend per month. What is it? If your take-home pay is $3,500 per week, it is $14,000 per month. If your grand total of monthly expenses is $12,000, you make more than you spend; if you spend $14,000 or more, you are on the edge or over and you need to make some adjustments.

GOD'S FORMULA FOR FINANCIAL FREEDOM

If for example, you earn more than you spend, we can flip ahead to investing and saving. Or you can stay here and work to make your margin better. In any case, you can, you really can, increase your earnings and at the same time, decrease your expenses. You can do this because you are looking at what you actually earn and what you truly spend. If you earn less than you spend, the first thing I suggest is that you look for ways to increase your income. Are you tithing and seeding? That is the very first thing, but you can also do some other things to make money as well. Please do not forget—cut the chains of credit card debt! Once you are no longer bound by high interest rates, you will probably find you have enough money to meet your expenses and have money left over for things like savings and investments.

When you start to think about earning more money, ask yourself things like, "Do I have something I could rent out? A pool? Maybe a spare room?" Do you have tools or machines you could rent out? Are you on land where you might plant something or sell something that could make money or give you an agricultural tax break? Do you have a marketable skill or knowledge? Can you tutor? Did you grow or have canned more vegetables than you need? Might they be sold? Is there wood on your land that might be sold? Could you be the neighborhood childcare service for a couple hours when your own kids are home? (There are limits on how many you can sit for before licensing regulations apply.) Is there someone in the neighborhood

MEET THE FINANCIAL YOU

who needs help with laundry? With shopping? With meal prep? In short, is there a side hustle that fits in with your routine? Keep your eyes open and ask God to help you see opportunities you might otherwise miss. If you are already doing the work, why not do just a bit more and get paid for it?

I personally am not a big fan of getting a second job but that is an option if it allows for sufficient family time. A decision to get a second job should be made in prayer and discussion with your spouse if you are married. If you are single, a second job may be just the place to meet people and make the money you need to make "ends meet" and have money left to allocate. Do not let yourself forget: You may be earning more, but you need every cent to break even and get to that important place where you can save and invest. Recognize your achievement when you get caught up. Be glad and grateful; praise God when you earn more and find ways to economize.

Take a hard look at your expenses. You can reduce what you spend. This will involve change, but it does not have to hurt. If your life becomes simpler, less hectic, your life can be less stressful. You can realize how fortunate, how blessed, you are to now see yourself financially secure. You can, with God's help, turn this change into an improved way of living. When trying to save money, you can look for clothing on sale or thrift shops for clothes and stay mindful of other things you want. Do you see a small appliance you need or a gift for a friend or relative? How about games and books or toys for kids? I do not want to get in trouble with Amazon, but why turn there when you can get the item you want, and need, for as little as a sixteenth of what it costs new? Is door-to-door delivery worth it? Remember to shop around for everything; the best rates on bank accounts and credit cards, the best/least expensive insurance, the least expensive cable or streaming package. How many channels do you need? Can you make do with less? Can your provider give you a better rate or do you need a new provider? Can you learn to do some simple home repairs? Do you need a manicure or a nail file and some polish?

Grocery shopping can be an art form and a terrific money saver. Thank God as you make your food list that you have the presence of mind to plan what you will buy. Shop weekly so that you will not miss the sales. Shop where the prices are the best. Look to places like bulk grocery stores. Stay out of quick marts and expensive coffee shops. Avoid high-end supermarkets. Make your own coffee or tea at home; get the thermos at a yard sale! Conserve paper products, use wash cloths and dish towels. Meal prep for the week, pack snacks and your lunch. Assemble your own snacks rather than buy those little pre-made packages. You get charged extra for that convenience. Get together with family and friends for celebrations at home, everybody can bring a dish, maybe exchange recipes. Maybe you will start to have at-home games or card nights; it is probably safer and saves on travel and tickets. Perhaps the kids will make new or better friends at home. Clip coupons and use them

MEET THE FINANCIAL YOU

for items your family will actually use or eat. Maybe you can join a coupon club at home or work. It can provide a new network of friends and add to the convenience of gathering coupons.

Flip some mental switches. Be proud of what you save. Be happy about money you do not spend. Set realistic budget goals and keep track of what you spend and save. Make your budget as realistic as you can. Do not shoot too high or too low. Pray about your budget goals. Nothing is a bargain if you do not need it or if you can get the same thing for free or significantly less. It is no sale if you do not need it. You do not have to go out to have a good time. What is the big deal about using washcloths and dish towels instead of consumable paper products? Open your heart and mind to God; appreciate what you have, and see new ways to earn and save.

Keep track of what you are doing financially. If the groceries for your family of four once cost $1,500 a month, what do they cost now that you shop around and do home prep? How far can you lower that bill? This is where a budget comes into play. A budget is the goal, the point where you want your spending to be. Maybe you want to lower your car repair bills and start to change your own oil. Or maybe it is still cheaper and better for you at a discount auto shop. Who knows until you check and budget. "Thank You, God, for showing me ways to economize. I am so grateful I saved while grocery shopping and made enough for supper and made mine and my spouse's lunch." Notice

GOD'S FORMULA FOR FINANCIAL FREEDOM

what groceries cost before you begin to economize. Set a new budget goal and work to reduce your grocery bill.

CHAPTER 8:

More Than One Kind of Savings

As soon as possible, and as early as you can, saving is one of the first things you do when you get your first job. You need to set up a regular savings account and let's not forget, the most important, a retirement account. I am so glad that I was able to find Scriptures in God's Word speaking about the importance of saving. I make sure that I maintain an emergency savings account not only for myself but for my family. If you do not have an emergency savings account, start one! You deserve peace of mind and the assurance that you can weather a period of unemployment or a broken water heater. Saving, because it is typically done automatically, is one of the easiest allocations you can make.

One of the things I found while going through the Bible, looking for Scripture that talks about saving, was the story of Joseph. He was used by God to interpret one of Pharaoh's dreams of the upcoming famine and told him there would be seven years of plenty that he needed to save up for so that the seven years of famine to follow would not only allow them to survive but to thrive (Genesis 41:28–32). One of the greatest takeaways from this story is not just about us saving and having emergency funds when things get difficult, but we, like Joseph, can thrive not just survive! The other Scripture verse I found in God's Word is found in Proverbs 21:20 (ESV), "Precious treasure and oil are in a wise man's dwelling, but a foolish man devours it." When I read this verse, I knew this was the verse I was looking for. Too many times I have found myself wanting to spend everything I had because it made me feel better about myself and lifted my self-esteem, only to find myself empty, broke, and still without friends. Maybe this is something you can relate to and have been dealing with in your own life. If so, there is hope for you. If God can heal my heart and reasons why I wasn't able to save money, God can help you too. I can give you all the tools and ways to save, but if you don't address the real reason on why you got into debt to begin with or why you can't save, because of hurt or past issues that you haven't turned over to God, none of this will help you get out of the pitfall of spending everything you have.

For starters, as part of your morning prayer or meditation, ask God to help you save. It can be as simple as saying, "God help me save money for emergencies." Or you may want to say more and plant your intention in your

MORE THAN ONE KIND OF SAVINGS

mind, to make it flourish in your life. You might say, "God, help me to do what You want me to do and to look for ways to save money. Help me to set money aside and not spend unnecessarily. Let me see victory in small daily savings. Let me notice where I have wasted money and let me put that cash aside as a safety net for my family. Show me ways to save and earn I may not yet have noticed. Help me to use the income You give me to save and keep my family and me out of debt. Wrap me in gratitude for the money I do not spend foolishly. Thank You for Your help. Amen." Pray regularly and aloud. Prayer, among other things, reinforces your intention and helps initiate habits.

If saving is new to you, look for activities and groups that help reinforce and strengthen this new habit. There is a spin-off group from Alcoholics Anonymous called Debtors Anonymous. I mention this because the group, like this book, wants you to learn to successfully manage your income and get out and stay out of credit card debt and hand-to-mouth existence.

Imagine the relief you will feel when you have a nest egg. When you praise God, when you say, "Thank You, God, for leading me to save and for helping my savings to grow. Thank You for strengthening me to save." Your confidence will grow when you thank God, when you praise Him. You can tithe, reduce your credit card debt, save, and earn more money all at the same time. Do what you can; just do not do nothing. Make your first goals short term and small. Then continue to build. When you have set aside

GOD'S FORMULA FOR FINANCIAL FREEDOM

the equivalent of three months' salary, see if you can make it six; then perhaps more? If you make $30,000 per year, you make $2,500 a month. For three months of backup emergency savings, you need $7,500. If you have a direct deposit for your salary, set it up so that 10 percent goes directly into your savings account. Unless you really look for it, this money will build without notice and you will save. When you find ways to cut back expenses, you can increase the amount you save or pay down debts quicker. Do this through automatic systems whenever you can. Let the fact that "you do not miss what you do not see" work to your advantage. Your reward is a steadily growing savings account. It is no easier or harder to save when you earn a lot or a little. I believe it is the enemy who tells you that you cannot save this much or that you cannot do without what some people see as normal everyday purchases. You do not have to do or spend like everyone else. For example, do some blind taste tests on name brand foods versus the store brand. Are they truly worth the extra dime a can or dollar a box? Little economies can result in big savings. Like Benjamin Franklin said "a penny saved is a penny earned"; nothing is too big or too little. Too many times we often feed our habits and not our healing.

Many of us at work buy coffee and a snack, or even lunch every day. Just look at the coffee alone. A cup can average between $2.50 to $5.00 and that is the low end. Beverages can average $3 per day. Three dollars times twenty workdays a month is $60/month or $720 per year.

MORE THAN ONE KIND OF SAVINGS

An inexpensive fast-food meal can range from $6–10 a day. I myself was purchasing breakfast and lunch every day. When I realized how much money I was wasting, I decided to get up earlier and eat breakfast at home and pack my lunch every day. The money I saved, I was able to start my emergency savings. The sooner you start, the better you will feel. Use your debit card to help you track these small daily purchases and you will notice frivolous spending. I would rather see this money in your account. According to Dawn Allcot, from Yahoo Finance, the average American spends $18,000 per year on non-essentials, in a survey by Ladder and One Poll and almost $3,800 is the average cost of impulse buys according to Ramsey solutions.[4]

What happens if you buy a filtered water pitcher and a reusable water bottle instead of plastic water bottles? You may begin prepping your lunches from meals you planned so that there would be leftovers. Maybe you also do some prepping when you make your Sunday meal. If we stop nickel and diming our money, most of us can put three to six months of savings in the bank in less than a year's time. When we can get rid of a bad habit and we economize, we will be able to save more than we've ever been able to, and yes, it's easier said than done. When you put these behaviors into practice, you will notice a change by spending less and saving more.

Another great way of saving is taking a look at the rates you're paying on your loans. You may be able to consolidate credit cards into a loan with a better interest rate or you may be able to refinance your auto loan. Just taking a few minutes out of your busy day can save you hundreds of dollars by restructuring your debt. I recently met a couple who was just starting out and they had financed their car at 19 percent for five years. Their credit had not yet been established when they first bought the car, and their credit score was low. Gradually they got better paying jobs and made regular payments on their car. They did not increase their debt. But the couple thought that because they had taken out a five-year loan at 19 percent that they were stuck with it. When they came to see me, I was able to offer them a new loan at 4.2 percent for the balance of their refinanced loan. That is a savings of almost 15 percent which equals thousands of dollars of savings. Even though interest rates are higher now, it's almost always a good idea to see if you can refinance. And guess what? Different banks offer different rates! Even more money saved. So, you may want to shop around.

At the time you establish a savings account, set up a retirement account. A retirement account can be set up with your employer, your bank, or even an investment firm. Of all allocations, saving may be the easiest to do. It can be straightforward; it does not require much study or research. You can save automatically. You can have your nest egg, your holiday club, your vacation club, and most importantly you can save for your retirement and not give it much thought. Set up a retirement account as soon as you begin to earn. Unless you are increasing your contribution, leave your retirement account alone until you are certain you are ready

MORE THAN ONE KIND OF SAVINGS

to retire. If your company has a matching program, then to the fullest extent possible, match it! If your company will match 3.5 percent, then you, if you can, put in 3.5 percent as well. That way you are saving 7 percent a year. If you are self-employed, I think I may have mentioned it, but start your own retirement fund for you and your employees, especially your employed family members. Your financial planner, or sometimes even your accountant, may be able to steer you toward good retirement firms or products. Or if you are good at investigating these things, you can find your own firm or retirement plan. Please keep in mind that when a firm is selling their product, what you are reading about them is mostly advertising. If you need to know how a firm or company is really doing, you need to access an independent review.

We all know by now that social security will not carry us through retirement and furthermore, that pensions are increasingly a thing of the past. With so much depending on our retirement savings and eventually our investment income, it is vital that we save as much as we can.

It is extremely important to have enough money to carry you through retirement. I have seen too many people have to come out of retirement to maintain their household due to inflation and cost of living expenses. Then I have heard people say that they are moving from one job to another, and they are withdrawing their retirement funds instead of rolling it over to their new employer. By withdrawing early from your retirement account, you will incur large amounts of taxes, penalties, and fees. So as soon as possible, if you have borrowed from your retirement account, do whatever you can to pay that back, as you are leaving a better rate of return off the table. I have met people who when they retire, sell their business, hoping to use the proceeds as a retirement fund. There are too many things that can go wrong with this plan. For one, businesses grow antiquated, outdated, and lose value. With change happening so rapidly, this is not the age to expect a thirty- or twenty-year-old business to grow in value as it gets older. It can, but typically, the opposite is true.

Some of us, and I include myself in this group, feel attacked by the enemy as we begin to manage our money, to tithe, to save. No matter how you choose to view it, it's only human to find it difficult to develop good habits. Saving money is one of the best habits you will ever develop. But just because God asks us to do things we know are good for us, does not mean it will be easy to do. Yes, it will be easier with God's help, but still, you are working against human nature, that "wants what you want when you want it." You may need a buddy or a support group to keep you on track. And marriage counseling may become an essential item for financial prosperity. If one partner wants to tithe and save and the other wants to spend and consume, there will be conflict and strife. Above all, pray for all the initiatives you are taking and recognize with praise and thanks everything that you do that will lead you to successful money management.

CHAPTER 9:

Eliminate Credit Card Debt

When you use the information in this book, you will have the money you need to live in abundance. No matter how broke you are right now, no matter how much credit card debt you have, you can start to form the habits you need to walk in God's promises for Financial Freedom. I wish I knew what I am about to share with you back in 2016. I was in over $55,000 in credit card debt and I had been unemployed. While it had nothing to do with my financial situation, my beloved mother died in July 2017. It added to my losses and grief. Without a job, I had to put my time and energy into a side hustle and make my living on stock market trades until I could find other employment. When I failed to follow God's Word about prosperity, I lost my footing, and I slipped financially. I crashed. I lost my investment and had to use credit cards for necessities, like food and shelter.

If you had met me then, you would not have been able to understand how I could get in such a mess. I had been in the financial industry since 2008. In addition to working two jobs, I had been going to school most of 2014–2016. I was working sixty-five hours a week and going to school at night. I knew a lot about finances and all the rules, regulations, and laws that governed money management. I even had some knowledge of how God wants us to prosper, but I did not apply it. And that was the mistake. I had loads of knowledge, but I was not applying it to the way God asks us to live, let alone living the way a financial advisor would instruct. I was living as I thought everyone else lived. I was deeply embedded in the American culture of hard work, education, and lots of self-gratification. I had gotten myself into a ton of debt by living like that. We had big celebrations on holidays. Nice clothes and lots of "things."

I may say it more than once in this book, but it is so important, it bears repeating. Once you have credit card debt you cannot afford, it only takes a moment to tip over into being unable to make a payment on time. Then the penalties, the late fees, the interest snowball, and everything comes crashing down. When it happens, it only takes a few days to fall apart. I want to say I thought I could handle credit cards. I knew how they worked. But instead of biting the bullet and saying I could not afford my life, I tried to prop myself and my family up, just until I could get back on my feet. I kept telling myself I would pay my credit card debt down, but instead I only got more cards and charged

ELIMINATE CREDIT CARD DEBT

more. It is a common mistake, but I was ashamed and disappointed with myself. That shame made the credit card problem even harder to deal with.

Somewhere, I found the strength to speak with a lawyer about filing bankruptcy. That meeting was pivotal in my own move to Financial Freedom. I knew, as did the lawyer, that once a person files bankruptcy, there is a strong probability that they will file for bankruptcy again and again. That is because credit cards are a bad habit. They are a bad, addictive habit. If we have the credit cards with us, in our wallets or purses, and we are accustomed to using them, we will use them again, and unless we put them in the bottom of our sock drawer or freeze them in a block of ice, we are likely to use them again. On the surface of things, they seem okay. Like I said, "Doesn't everybody use credit cards?" And that is true. According to Lyle Daly from fool.com, almost 82 percent of all Americans use credit cards and credit card debt.[5] According to Jacob Wade, and gobankingrates survey, nearly half of Americans have savings of less than $500 and nearly 60 percent of Americans have less than $1,000 saved.[6] From where I sit now, I know those fellow Americans are on the brink of disaster or may have already fallen off a few times. It is very hard to see bad credit card use as the dangerous habit it is. Especially when the problem is yours and you know what you are doing, don't you? You really need that new dishwasher or that big truck. Who knows when you will need to haul something? It looks like everyone else has

GOD'S FORMULA FOR FINANCIAL FREEDOM

decent things and uses credit cards. They do not seem to have a problem. We tell ourselves, "I can certainly manage my credit cards." Or "I'll just use my cards a little, just to get the bonus rewards or my discount." Or "I must have a car and I need new tires. Just this once I will use my card." As a person with financial training, someone who should have known better and as a person who still works in finances, take my word for it, people in the US are NOT managing their credit cards. Credit card debt can happen to anyone, and it is an epidemic.

I felt awful. I had worked so hard, done all the "right" things. It was not fair. I was angry. I was ashamed. I had to admit defeat.

The bankruptcy lawyer told me he thought I was someone who could get out of the credit card use habit. He told me, "You are smart enough to know this does not define you; you will bounce back and overcome all this." He was sincere and I felt it. I believed him. Those words of encouragement meant so much to me. His words gave me confidence. My losses were about so much more than money. My self-esteem took a terrible hit. That man, whom I respected, turned around and showed me respect. I tell you, the reader, from the bottom of my heart, as you read this book, I know you can do it too. If I could be in the room with you, I would tell you, "You can break the credit card habit. You can recover from your credit card debt. You will not be a statistic."

ELIMINATE CREDIT CARD DEBT

With the lawyer's guidance, I filed for bankruptcy, Chapter 13, which specifically applies to credit card debt. That should tell you something right there; credit card debt is so widespread, such an epidemic, that a special category of bankruptcy, Chapter 13, had to be created just for credit card indebtedness. It also suggests that for the big corporations, there is a lot of money to be made from peoples' need to buy what they want, when they want it, when they *think* they need it. Even after you file for bankruptcy, you are often asked to apply for new, fresh cards. The banks and corporations do not think anyone is a particularly good risk for a credit card. Sometimes I suspect they want the person who has a bad track record. All the financial institutions know is that there is a lot of money to be harvested from people who buy when they cannot afford it. If you have or are about to file bankruptcy, you have demonstrated that you will be one of those people. Fresh cards are then issued with interest rates as high as 30 percent or higher. And because they are credit cards, you can walk into any store and with that card, you can charge something and convince yourself it belongs to you. While the card is not maxed out, you can tell yourself that what you charged is a small item, only $25. It does not cross your mind that when this $25 is added to your indebtedness, you may pay as much as $75 for that "inexpensive" item by the time you truly own it. Your debt, once acquired, may last for as much as twenty years. And the process repeats itself. Day after day. A person sometimes charges things before they can afford it because they *really* need it or they see something appealing and think they need "just a little treat." The amount owed builds and the interest compounds and before a person realizes, they cannot pay their day-to-day bills or their credit card debt. That individual then loses everything. Just as I did.

I want you to know, you are a smart person too. For starters, you bought this book, didn't you? Not because it was inexpensive, or I was the author, but because you wanted to be financially free. You can learn to manage your money in ways that make credit cards take a back seat. You do not have to learn the hard way. I am excited for you. You can be free of not only credit card debt but bad debt entirely! You can make more money and keep all of it for yourself and your family! It will take effort and the formation of new habits, but you can do it. You are worth the effort.

A. AVOID THE CREDIT CARD TRAP

Right now, in the United States, you must have a good credit rating, or score, to make most big purchases and have a low credit interest rate. That means we all must use credit cards. As we turn eighteen, we begin to get offers for credit cards. They usually have a limit of about $500 unless they are used for a student loan. Student loans, by the way, are another can of worms to be avoided, if possible. For now, we will talk about just plain old credit cards. My first advice to you concerning credit cards is do not use them if

ELIMINATE CREDIT CARD DEBT

you cannot pay them off every month. And secondly, shop around. When you can, get the ones with the best rates and no or low user fees. Low rates mean you pay less interest, not that you ever want to carry an item on your account long enough to be charged interest. But for the rest of your life, for as long as you use credit cards, seek the cards with the lowest interest rates and no carrying charges. While you may not use every card you own, it is a good idea not to close the cards. Closing credit cards reduces your credit score. But when you first start out, it is hard to imagine why you might need more than three credit cards.

When you are a young adult, the credit card companies offer you cards and charge high interest rates because they do not know how you will use your card. That credit card that arrived in the mail when you were eighteen was no gift. It was bait. You may not be able to handle indebtedness. I suspect the corporations hope young people will not know how to handle credit cards because if that young person charges more than they can pay off, the credit card company stands to make a lot of money from the interest that young adults owe. Because of youth and inexperience, you are labeled a "risk." You are untested and someone who may not be able to pay enough, pay on time, or be someone who may default and not be able to make the payments! Try to keep in mind that the credit card company makes its money in the interest they charge you. The more you charge, the more they make. And the sooner you pay for your purchases, the less they make. So, they like your indebtedness. A lender likes a young, inexperienced debtor with a high interest rate. You make THEM money. You may be a bad risk, someone who continues to run up charges and develop a high debt-to-income ratio. All that means is that when you have a high debt-to-income ratio, there comes a point in time when you will not earn enough money to pay off your debt in about a year or less. You, in fact, may be someone who owes more money than you can reasonably expect to pay off in a couple of decades. It is this debt-to-income ratio that primarily determines your credit score; not, as most people think, whether your payments have been made on time.

As your indebtedness grows, so too does the amount of interest owed. Gradually, but in as little as a year's time, you can find yourself in a situation where almost your entire monthly payment is going toward the interest, not the principal owed. For example, you may easily come to owe $15,000 in credit card debt, and your interest rate might be 24 percent. The credit card company may ask for a minimum of $400 per month. The company mentions in small print that if you make the minimum payment, it will take you fifteen or even twenty years to pay off that card. Remember, of that $400 monthly payment as little as $25 or $30 will be applied to the principal or actual balance; the rest of what you pay is in interest! The credit card company is making money like crazy and in a very short time has made enough profit to cover any loss should you fail to pay monthly. It may not sound too bad if you quickly read it but look at it another way. The credit card company is making $375 per month from you or $4,500 per year. You, on the other hand, have only paid the amount owed on $15,000, down by $300 in that same years' time, and if you do not charge anything else, your total amount owed has only been reduced to $14,700. You may want to re-read this paragraph for motivation. Better still, re-read your credit card statement if you already have one.

As we mature, we assume more responsibilities: car payments, rent, groceries, utility bills, and these bills are pretty much necessities. If you do not pay these basic bills, you will struggle greatly. Naturally these bills get paid first if you can, but what if you do not pay that $400 credit card bill? Then next month it is double, and there are late fees and interest penalties. Now that next monthly credit card bill is $900, not $400. My math on this is not perfect but what I am telling you is true. If you could not afford an on-time monthly payment, how are you going to pay double that amount plus a late fee the next month? Some people open new credit cards to make payments on existing credit cards. How smart is that? Many of us tell ourselves we will catch up, spend less, or get another job. Those are the things we needed to do BEFORE we charged anything. We tell ourselves we will use our income tax refund to pay off our credit cards. That seldom happens. If we have the credit card habit, we use cards every week. A tax return only comes once a year. That single annual return is no match for regular credit card use.

GOD'S FORMULA FOR FINANCIAL FREEDOM

Please, do not get me wrong, it's okay to use credit cards wisely; in fact we must establish a credit rating. But do not make more purchases than you can pay off every month. Put money in an emergency savings account for that inevitable "big" expense, like new tires or a broken water heater. Get no more than three good credit cards, the best has the lowest interest rates and no annual fee. This is all so simple to say; so hard to do. I can only promise you it gets easier with time and practice.

I already told you that I did not follow my own advice. I used credit cards to pay for my living expenses. What I should have done before I used a credit card to pay a single electric bill or mortgage payment was to change my lifestyle the way I did after I filed for bankruptcy. After I filed Chapter 13, I lived with less and went without the conveniences and nice new things to which I thought I was entitled. Things I thought I needed. I could have spared myself a seven-year ordeal if I had bitten the bullet when I first lost my job. But in my career, I had a brief period of success and experienced a dramatic increase in income. When I suddenly lost it, I convinced myself I could recapture that time and lifestyle. Some of the biggest things I learned from that personal fall were that there was a lot of extraordinary pressure that contributed to my mistake, and that while I should have known better, God still loved me, and I was smart enough to recover. Above almost anything else, I want you to know that you too can jump in and manage your credit cards at any time. It isn't easy. While

I hope you can avoid my mistake, if you find you are over your head in credit card debt, let us talk about what you can do to recover.

B. BEFORE CHAPTER 13

It is possible that you may be in a position that allows you to avoid bankruptcy. If you can avoid it, you should. But if you need to file, then it's also important to do that too. Just to be transparent, there are three types of bankruptcy, but in these chapters, we are only talking about Chapter 13, which specifically applies to credit card debt. You may be able to avoid filing if the following conditions exist for you:

1. You can consolidate your credit card debt into one payment with a bank or a debt consolidation company like "Accredited," "AVANT," or "Upstart."

2. You can make changes in your lifestyle and payment schedules that will reasonably keep you from having to incur new debts. You can lock up your credit cards and NOT use them.

3. You have or can increase your income so that you have enough money to cover your living expenses—your mortgage or rent, utilities, groceries, medical bills or medical insurance, clothing, transportation, maybe childcare. You can pay more than minimum payment and pay off one

GOD'S FORMULA FOR FINANCIAL FREEDOM

card at a time. (Take your time when figuring this out because you want to capture every legitimate expense you have. And you will want to pare down or get rid of unnecessary expenses.)

4. Then you must ask: Will my actual income (not my hoped-for income) cover my total living expenses, allow me to save for a rainy day, plus that onetime consolidated monthly credit card payment? Now, if you have enough to put aside a little savings in case of emergency, that is smart, prudent. And if there is a bit more, you can pay directly on the credit card debt principal. Lucky you! Then you have a fair chance of bringing your credit card debt under control without filing bankruptcy.

As you are putting this factual list of actual income and expenses together, it's not a bad idea to sit down with a financial advisor or a financially savvy trusted friend or relative. An impartial eye will help you decide whether you can manage your bills and your credit. You may find other areas where you can cut expenses. If you are working on that example and have $15,000 in credit card debt, it may take you five years to eliminate it. Five years with no fresh credit charges. When you are about two years into this recovery plan, call your credit card lender and ask if you might be eligible for a lowered interest rate. It is timely payments on manageable balances that earn you improved credit scores and lowered interest rates. Now shop around

ELIMINATE CREDIT CARD DEBT

and see if another company or bank might want to take on your loan at an even lower rate. You might be pleasantly surprised and maybe you might satisfy your indebtedness ahead of schedule, say in four years instead of five; save yourself hundreds if not a couple thousand dollars in interest.

All the while, you are paying on this consolidated credit card debt; through a debt consolidation loan, you are improving your credit score. In those first two years, you may move from a rating of 610 (poor risk/high interest rate) to a 710. Then you will be eligible for a lowered interest rate and as a result be able to make "more effective" payments—payments that allow you to tackle principal, not just pay your lender a lot of interest.

While you do all this, there will be lots of families who appear to have more than you. You may experience some actual withdrawal when you take your credit cards out of your wallet or purse and put them in a safe place, maybe in a lockbox in your closet. Ask God to help you remember it takes at least thirty days to establish new ways of doing things. I suspect it may take even longer to break bad habits. The advertisements and infomercials will tell you that you need things you didn't know you wanted until you saw them on your TV or cell phone. Your kids, if you have them, will want gifts and candy and snacks and things like the other kids. You, because you are a "good" parent, will want to give them as much as you can. Just make sure it is what you can realistically afford. Do not do what your credit card company wants you to do—to spend. To "owe." Keep in mind that we are so blessed to put food on the table and have warm, clean beds to sleep in. If you are not doing it, sit down to meals together and say grace. Yes, it is a time to thank God for His goodness, but it's also a reminder that making ends meet is a blessing.

C. BANKRUPTCY

If you find yourself in a position where bankruptcy is your only option, after doing everything you can to avoid it, then these are some things you may want to know. Depending on what kind of bankruptcy you do, this may last up to seven years and may not allow you to get any new forms of credit during this time period, including buying a new car, getting a credit card, and buying a home. There are options out there to help you establish new credit during this time period, such as applying for a secured credit card. Where you have funds in a savings account to back the credit card limit. If you do need to apply for an auto loan during this time period, there will be a high interest rate which can hinder your Financial Freedom journey. I would highly recommend purchasing a vehicle for cash instead.

Abiding by the requirements of my bankruptcy recovery period was grueling, but during this time, I formed some conservative habits. I make it a practice to continue to use no more than three credit cards. I continue to pay each one of them off at the end of the month. I believe that this recovery has been due to my daily faithfulness to the Word of God. I find myself refreshed and strengthened by devotions and prayer. I would not have come this far this fast without the help of God. I truly pray that you will combine these sound devotional and financial practices in your own life.

I will not spend much time talking about this topic, as I believe that this may be a short season in your life and does not apply to everyone. If you find yourself having to make this hard decision, there is help out there to get you back on track in your financial journey. I know this may be a hard season for you, as it was for myself, but please know that now looking back, it was a short time in my life, and I was able to learn new spending and saving habits. You will come out of this better than going in, and you can use this time to learn and grow in your financial understanding. By making these changes, you will be creating better financial decisions and lower your chances of needing to file bankruptcy again.

CHAPTER 10:

Ways to Make Money

You can meet your financial needs in a lot of ways. From a previous chapter, you learned that you can cut expenses. You can also make more money. You can earn more and save on expenses *at the same time*. You can save, invest, get a better job, and you can cultivate "passive" streams of income. If you currently have a lot of expenses, it can be difficult to gather money together to invest or avoid credit card debt. It is easiest to keep things modest and small when you are young and first start out. Can the kids share a room? Can you make do with one car or a used car? Can the heater be set a little lower in the winter, the air a little higher in the summer? Once you acquire a standard of living, it can be hard to step back. Give it your best shot. Because if you are spending every penny you earn to stay afloat, it will be hard, not impossible, but hard to get ahead. When you carve back on expenses, you will feel the initial cut, but you will also gain room to function.

This chapter explains ways to increase your income

and enhance your financial stability. *God's Formula for Financial Freedom* prepares you to be open to success, to recognize and acknowledge events as opportunities. You are so much more likely to prosper if you persevere with the *formula* even if your investment process may appear to you to go in stops and starts. You will do better when you see yourself as a winner and are convinced God loves and supports you. When you realize that God cares about how you use money, that the gift of money is actually from God, you will want God's direction before you do anything with the money you are given. Pray before you invest and never invest on impulse. Pray before you make purchases. Thank God when money comes into your life. God *does care* how you use the money you receive. He wants to see you use money to fulfill His intentions for you. Reading this book will help you do exactly that. When you acknowledge God as the provider, Jehovah Jireh, then yes, you honor God when you tithe. You also properly respect and use the funds you are given. We should ask God for guidance and direction for how He wants us to use His finances, and we should pray before making any financial decisions. This prayer is one way to ask God for guidance in this area: "God, I know You will use Your portion to Your greater glory, and I will use the money You give me as carefully as I can. I want to know how You want me to use my funds. Inspire my use of money. Thank You for giving me that knowledge. Amen." You are positioned to grow. The amazing thing about God's love is that no matter where you are on your financial path, you can always move

WAYS TO MAKE MONEY

onto the pathway to Financial Freedom. You can always use God's Formula.

Another reminder: God's blessings are not subject to Bernie Madoff's Ponzi schemes or recessions or the vagaries of the stock market. I hear an old hymn in my mind when I write this, "On Christ, the solid Rock, I stand, all other ground is sinking sand."[7] Secondly, this book explains how, when you stand with God, in His favor, you can expect to earn, save, and invest. When you move in faith you see opportunities with regularity. That is exciting. Things are not such a struggle, not as frightening. You have the strength and support to try again, to try another way. When you see yourself on the path God wants for you, then you are on a road that can lead to generational wealth.

Once you have the equivalent of three months' or more worth of paycheck/income tucked away in savings and about ten to fifteen thousand set aside in a dedicated nest egg, you can begin to invest. (You may feel comfortable investing at the same time you save; that is your decision; just decide prayerfully.) You typically can explore any or all of five customary income streams on your path to prosperity. I also want you to expect unexpected blessings. We are not necessarily talking about winning the lottery, but I have no intention of saying what God can or cannot do. I just know that God is faithful and rewards His faithful servants. Therefore, in addition to God's blessings, the income streams you can nourish are the following:

107

GOD'S FORMULA FOR FINANCIAL FREEDOM

1. A steady job with the opportunity to earn a decent salary. (Where you can make more money than it costs you to live.)

2. One or more side hustles; the more you enjoy this vocation, the better. It can grow from a hobby like wood carving or a skill, and it can grow from a hobby to a business. Some people have more than one side hustle.

3. A portfolio of investments, stocks, bonds, mutual funds, etc. You can invest by yourself or through a firm. Prepare thoroughly before you invest.

4. Rental properties/real estate.

5. Land or collectables. (Owning land may also aid in lowering your taxes and provide agricultural tax breaks.) You may even look at gold, silver, or even things like Rolex watches.

There are occasions when these five areas overlap or may not be active all at the same time. Who knows how far a job may take you. If you see value in your work, if you work conscientiously, you have an excellent chance of having your work valued and rewarded. As a conscientious worker, you will probably help make profits for your company's business; you may inspire others, suggest improvements, etc. On the other hand, if you are self-employed and "right with God," you can also flourish. If your contributions are not recognized, then you will have the self-esteem and strength to start over or move on to where what you offer is appreciated. Keep in mind that no job is too small. Cleaning ladies have become cleaning companies.

Some people may only use one or two income streams as they move toward Financial Freedom. For example, there may come a time when you have enough money from dividends so that you no longer need to work. Then your focus may shift to managing your investments. A job is usually something you need when you first begin to build your investment fund and climb the ladder of success. If the paycheck is not quite good enough or the rise to success not fast enough, then a side hustle can be helpful, often essential in the building of investment capital. Or even if your dividends or other income streams pay sufficiently, you may like or grow to enjoy your vocation, your job. If you do, then you can work at it, typically, for as long as you like. Just tuck the thought away that most multimillionaires do not work a nine to five job; if anything, they cultivate the interest and dividends from their investments.

You may also find that two income streams merge into each other. You and perhaps your partner may have two different skill sets. This could mean you have complementary side hustles. One of you may be knowledgeable about construction or building trades. The other one may be versed in real estate or home decorating. Those are complementary skill sets for rehabilitating homes and reselling them. If one of you has some presentation skills, then you may be looking at a TV show or maybe a podcast. The trick here is to stay awake to what you like to do and ways to use your own interests, abilities, and inclinations to provide a marketable skill, service, or product. If one of you is a teacher and the other a musician, then who knows what the two of you might come up with. Would your friends in the orchestra appreciate it if you arranged a space, a conveniently located room, for musical instrument training? Could some teaching be offered over the Internet? Will you set up the advertising that brings in new music students? All occupations have so many aspects and potential avenues of diversification, sharing, and marketing, that even a single job may launch you into multiple income streams.

Each of the five sources can benefit from your study or training, effort and often an affiliation with a mentor. It is a good idea to look for the people who are contributing or working successfully and mimic them. You can find tips and inspiration if you read about someone who has succeeded, like Warren Buffett, and couple this with explanatory textbooks and your own personal practice or drill. Investing in the stock market is complicated and can require real study, practice, and exposure, especially if you plan to be self-reliant. Give yourself time to learn and start small. When you first begin, you will probably want to balance your investments between conservative safer investments like IRAs, bonds, and mutual funds and then put a small amount, not much more than 5 percent of your investment monies into some chancier well-researched

WAYS TO MAKE MONEY

stocks. With time and experience, stock investment can increase.

Sources 3, 4, and 5 (investments, real estate, and rentals) are sometimes called *passive streams* of income. Most truly wealthy people make most of their income from passive investments. A lot of folks want to amass enough dividend income from investments so that they can retire comfortably and use only a portion of their dividends. Ideally, even in retirement, they want to reinvest some of their return so that the original investment can continue to grow, to prosper.

A passive stream of income, at start-up, needs your oversight but usually, once established, not your labor. There can be several passive streams of income—a rental property, maybe an index fund, or dividend paying stock— even person-to-person lending. Even though there may be some debate about whether it's okay to be a lender or a borrower, most of us already borrow in some way or another. I think personal lending between private individuals can be beneficial to both investors and borrowers. Especially if you know the borrower, it may be worth a look. There are websites that list people who are looking for loans, sometimes for start-up companies. Usually, the advantage to the borrower is that they can get the loan at a lower rate of interest, while for the lender, they can lend the money at a higher rate than they might earn from an established firm. Another passive stream of money, particularly if you have enough money, may be to "gift" a family member up to $10,000 with no tax for the recipient or gift giver. This can only be done yearly. There are times when such gifts can help keep wealth "in the family." Or such a gift can certainly kick-start a college education or small business start-up.

There are many types of bonds: I-bonds, government bonds, municipal bonds, even corporate bonds. Bonds usually have lower rates of return than stocks, but the returns are locked-in, guaranteed for a specified number of months or years. Bonds are safer than stocks but typically have a lower rate of return. However, if the company or corporation who issued the bonds collapses, then the bonds can fail. Typically, however, bonds are known for their durability. If you are new to the stock market or nearing retirement, bonds can be a good investment, perhaps the best one.

There is so much to the stock market. For example, some stocks do better in a recession while others do better in a time of inflation. You might want to know and understand something about micro and macroeconomics. And while right now the dollar is strong, this makes it an even trickier time to invest in the stock market. With gas and oil prices sharply rising, production and shipping is more costly, and this is called a "head wind." You can read a few chapters on what this means to you as an investor. And yet, another important stock market behavior is that as interest rates go up, people look to hedge funds and banks look to invest in fixed interest investments where they can get a guaranteed rate of return. When banks do this, it is called a "flight to safety." When we see this coupled with rising federal interest rates and layoffs in big companies, this can be seen as some indicators of recession. If unemployment numbers climb as well, then recession is even more likely. Stocks are risky and understanding the complexities of stock investing can be difficult. Still, even if you plan to go with a firm, learn something about the market so that you can keep an eye on what your agent is doing.

If you cannot resist the market, start small and do not invest more in stocks than you can afford to lose. There are trading platforms that allow you to invest in tens and hundreds of dollars. With trades like this, you are buying in fractions. A few years ago, you had to buy in blocks of 100 shares or more and access to the market was expensive, easily in the tens of thousands of dollars. It was too much for the average person. It is still safer and wiser to play, to pretend or practice tracking the rise and fall of stocks you like than to practice with actual purchases. But you may be someone who absorbs stock market dos and don'ts quickly. Even then, keep it small, and preferably use your newfound skills to follow your investment firm. Monitor your firm, get to know them, and from them, see what they do. If you cannot resist the market, just know you are not alone. When investment firms made investing available to everyone, the stock market burgeoned, in fact, grew astronomically. One more feature of the market is the influence of politics and upcoming elections that can cause volatility in the market short term, and this can be seen as a great time to invest for the long term.

When you are in a rising rate economy, one where interest rates keep going up, investors will move away from growth stocks and move toward *value* stocks, stocks that have fixed dividends and high rates of return. Right now, the market is being driven in some large part by fear and greed. Investors are watching their stocks very closely, especially people who self-direct their own holdings. When the stock market is going down more than going up, it can be known as a bear market that can last for up to eighteen months. While this is happening, it can be a great time to get into a scheduled investment plan and make weekly or bi-weekly purchases depending on how often you get paid. Use this time period of purchasing to lower your average on share prices while increasing your position to prepare for a market reversal and make more money on your investments. Set a goal for when the market reverses to know when to sell your stocks and make a profit. The time for beginner investments can come at any time. In the meantime, you might look at buying some bonds on your own. *Treasurydirect.gov* has I bonds which are better than most CDs and certainly better than an ordinary bank account.

Alternatively, you may hire a financial advisor. The problem here is that most firms expect a minimum start-up investment amount of at least $100,000. They also charge fees for their expertise and service. That is why

WAYS TO MAKE MONEY

you may need the combined earnings of a job and a side-hustle. Once you have sufficient capital, sufficient money to invest, these firms can help you build your wealth, create your "portfolio" for you. But I always recommend that you shop around for an investment advisor and acquire some investment know-how of your own.

Now, whether or not you decide to move into real estate, there is nothing wrong with learning something about that field as well. If you get training, you will have the advantage of knowing the terminology, i.e., how to talk the *lingo*. It does not take long, and honestly, it is not as difficult as learning how to invest in the stock market. You may even want to become licensed. With experience, you learn things such as which real estate companies have a good reputation for being fair, honest, and making profitable sales and responsible purchases. Then you are in a position not only to see for yourself but to see as your brokerage firm "sees." That puts you in a position to acquire properties, maybe even properties you want to rehabilitate and sell. You will be in a better position to move and use properties as they become available. Being first on the scene is an important, valuable vantage point. Working with a real estate firm will also help you learn the benefits of renting and owning.

The rules for investing and saving differ for those of you who work for a business or agency as opposed to being self-employed. For example, if you work for someone, you will probably want a 403B or 401K. If your employer does contribution matching, you will absolutely want to

GOD'S FORMULA FOR FINANCIAL FREEDOM

contribute as much as they will match. That means if they match up to 3.5 percent and you put in your share, also 3.5 percent, your total investment will be 7.0 percent. That is an opportunity you do not want to miss, especially nowadays when there are seldom any pensions and social security is not nearly enough to live on in retirement. If you are self-employed, your business is often considered your nest egg. It is sometimes thought of as your retirement money which you collect when you retire and sell your business. A small business can be difficult to keep up-to-date and can become obsolete. So even if you are self-employed, it is not a bad idea to get your own privately held IRA. If you are self-employed, absolutely ask your tax advisor or accountant where your retirement holdings need to be.

I like to think I have pointed you in several directions, any of which can lead to wealth. When you follow these guidelines and make enough money to meet your living needs, save and invest, then you have the sources of successful cash streams. I also hope I have emphasized how important it is to get the training, exposure, and expertise you need to move ahead with actual investments and purchases. Follow what interests you the most.

CHAPTER 11:

How to Allocate

If you are trapped in credit card debt or your cost of living exceeds your income, then you will not have enough money to allocate funds for saving and investing. That is why we talked about how to get out of debt and live within your means before we arrived at these pages. These two steps precede investing. Debt and living expenses can take a big bite out of your ability to save and invest. That does not mean it cannot be done. However, the credit card indebtedness must stop. Living inside your income can be one of the hardest things a person can do. It is yet another reason why I pray that you will rely on God and let Him strengthen you. If you do not do it already, living within your means will probably require you to make more money AND reduce your spending. Things that may seem essential to your way of life, you may have to sacrifice. You may have to rent or live with family. You may want to make do with one car, even if this means public transportation or carpooling. Grocery shopping and meals will have to be preplanned, and try to stick to sales or coupons when possible. Have your meals prepared or cooked at home. Instead of congratulating yourself every time you find a sale, pat yourself on the back every time you do not buy something, every time you do without or get the thing you think you need for free. It is much easier to carve back expenses before you are married or have children. Still, I believe you can do it. Even if you must build your saving strategy a little at a time. You can, one foot in front of the other, economize. Even while you cut back in other areas, tithe as much as you can, up to the full 10 percent.

When you tithe and give as outlined here in *God's Formula*. I am confident that you will make more money than it costs you to live. The strategies for credit card debt reduction will work. When you make more than you spend on your lifestyle then you can allocate your money into tithing, saving, retirement, investing and your daily living expenses. When your income exceeds your living expenses this is a benchmark, a turning point. It is definitely a time to praise God. You might say:

> *Thank You, God, for helping me get out of debt and for helping me find ways to earn more and cut expenses. Thank You for helping my family in this challenging effort. I am especially grateful for the unexpected blessings You have given me. Thank You for strengthening my commitment to tithe and helping me see ways to meet the 10 percent. I know You will help me to allocate money to saving and investing. Help me to set*

HOW TO ALLOCATE

reasonable expectations for myself and to notice when You reward my efforts!

Thank You for all the good things You have already given me and help me to stay open to the blessings yet to come! Amen.

Now you can begin to allocate your income with these goals in mind:

10 percent to *God* (your actual church)

10 percent to your *savings* (as paycheck and emergency backup)

10 percent to *retirement fund*

10 percent to *investing*

60 percent to *cost of living* (which may include monthly credit card payoff and buy down)

The total allocation will equal all or 100 percent of your annual income. Your allocation will change as your income increases, and you can look at the figures monthly, take your financial pulse, and actually notice what is going on. In the very beginning, you may have to lower your initial percentages from 10 percent to 5 percent or even lower. You may need the help of a financial advisor or the advice of a savvy friend. Do not stop tithing and seeding, even if at first your ability to invest may be small. Keep track of the money that comes your way and look for ways to increase it. As your income increases, you will have the opportunity to invest more, not spend more. Your cost of living, if you keep your purchases and expenses modest, will not eat up an unfair share of your total income.

As your income increases, and it will, you can allocate more to each area. When investment grows, there is every reason to believe that so will your income. At first, when your allocation for investment is small, your return from investment will not be big. That is why we look to other income sources, especially at first. Here again, I wish these allocations and numbers were taught in public school and as part of Sunday school and worship. People need to know this information before they get caught up in debt or accustomed to living beyond their means.

The goal is to lower your cost of living by paying off debts as soon as possible; the sooner the better as this will allow you to allocate more funds toward retirement and investing. By getting out of debt as soon as possible, you can start creating saving habits; the money you were using for your credit card bill can now be placed in savings. This is almost like giving yourself a raise by having more money each month by lowering your debts. Credit cards should be a focus and priority, as the biggest wealth inhibitor is credit card debt because of the high interest rates. As you increase your cash flow, you will have more money to use for retirement and investing to earn more income. Once you have enough savings, you can start putting additional funds toward your mortgage. The profits you make from

HOW TO ALLOCATE

investing, you can also put toward your mortgage as an additional principal payment that can save you thousands of dollars for the life of the loan.

Once you can get your living expenses under 50 percent, you can start using extra funds toward seeding. By allocating extra funds toward seeding, monies used to sow into God's kingdom, you will see your investments, saving, and checking grow exponentially to where you never thought possible. Take it from me; it has happened. I have never had a better rate of return on earthly investments than what I've been able to receive from God.

Conclusion

I really hope and pray that you will put this into practice as you live out your financial journey toward Financial Freedom. You will be tested, and you may want to throw in the towel and have seasons of financial trial, but you will overcome them with God and reminding yourself of His promises found in His Word. If you find yourself not being able to tithe, you can start by almsgiving. This is only a small step in the right direction; use this as a way to start your new financial foundation. It may take a leap of faith and include sacrifice to get you to tithe 10 percent but know that when you do, God will meet your needs (Philippians 4:19). I have heard many people say that they can't tithe due to financial conditions. I say to you that there are ways to eliminate unnecessary expenses to allow you to be in obedience to God. Through tithing, this will allow you to overcome inflation and recession in your life. When wanting to move up in your career and get promoted, don't forget about acknowledging God through your firstfruits. And finally, the overflow and living in the abundance of God comes from sowing financial seeds, which is over and above the 10 percent tithe.

This is an important part but please don't forget that you then need to tend and take care of those seeds. It takes watering those seeds through prayers of affirmations and then feeding those seeds with prayers of thanksgiving for what God is going to do. When those thoughts of doubt and worry come into your mind, reject them immediately and definitely don't ponder or meditate on them as they can and will become weeds in your financial field and delay your harvest. Only you can abandon your seeds and stop the process of your harvest. Don't let this be you! I know many people may consider this the prosperity message, but I consider this the financial formula that has changed my life and has given me more time to share with family and friends and not have to live paycheck to paycheck.

By no means is this formula a "get rich quick," but if you give with an open heart and follow this as a guide for your finances, you will reap an abundant harvest in due time. Remember you can't out give God! Everything will be in God's timing, and you will have to have faith to see it come to pass. When you build your financial house on the promises of God, you will be able to withstand the storms of life, knowing that you will reap a harvest if you faint not (Galatians 6:9–10). The world system puts much emphasis on the financial house but spends no time talking about the foundation which it's built on. Only through God's Word can we see that everything must be built on a solid foundation (Matthew 7:24–27). Once we do this, then we can apply all these other things that we learn about finances into our lives, which is the financial house with many rooms. My dad would always tell me when I was young, "Finances will either change you, or you will change what it can do."

CONCLUSION

With God's formula as our foundation and the things taught in this book as our house, we can be that city on a hill that can't be hidden and a testimony of God's goodness and blessings in our life (Matthew 5:14). My desire is that you will see finances in a different perspective and have a cheerful heart ready and willing to be used by God. I hope this book brings you Financial Freedom that allows you to be able to spend more time with family and friends and be able to leave an inheritance for your children's children (Proverbs 13:22). And finally, my prayer for you is that you will be blessed to be a blessing. This is not for us to store and hoard but to make a lasting impact and change in the lives of all those that we come in contact with through the way we live our Financial Freedom!

If you have read this book and have not already accepted Jesus Christ as your Lord and Savior, I would love to tell you that this is the best decision I have ever made in my life. All you have to do is say, "Dear Jesus, I admit I am a sinner and believe that You died on the cross for my sins and rose three days later. I ask You to forgive me of my sins and I want You to come into my heart, change me, and I want You to be my Lord and Savior." If you said that prayer, you are now saved and on your way to heaven. Find the nearest church, tell someone there that you recently accepted Christ, and they will help you grow in your newfound life.

Testimonials

I was born into poverty and low income, so my knowledge of finances has been minimal. Through Mr. Barbetto's curriculum, I learned to plant seeds, have faith, and be expectant of their growth. God has shown up and out for my family in a life-changing way while going through this curriculum. I believe the spirit of poverty and lack has been broken off of us and their families for generations to come in Jesus' name! I'm so thankful I didn't stay stuck in the broken record of what I knew, and with Rodney's guidance, I don't ever have to find myself there again. Jesus wants to be involved in every part of our lives including our finances. If you're unsure what that would look like, read this book and allow the Holy Spirit to move in ways you never dreamed possible.

Thank you again, Rodney! May the Lord bless you and your family all the days of your life!

– Sandra H

Rodney was able to give us tools of wisdom, not only for everyday life but for our spirit. We've learned the true meaning of tithing, firstfruit, alms, and sowing a seed. Latoya was able to take the lessons learned about tithing and see change. Taking the money from her net income instead of her gross she has seen a growth in income. There are times when we all have second guessed giving our tithes. But with the words spoken and the scriptures given it strengthened our faith. He has led us down the right path in our financial journey. Through it all, TRUST IN GOD, HE IS OUR ULTIMATE PROVIDER!

It has truly been a blessing to be able to obtain the knowledge he has given us.

– Paul M & Latoya M

This was the exact information I needed to change the course of my lineage forever. Because of these principles expressed in the text, I can boldly say I have sound financial direction rooted in biblical principles that has not only affected my life but also the lives of people that God has held me responsible for. I am beyond grateful to stumble upon this information and believe this book will play a huge role in God's people claiming back the abundance and dominion that was given in the beginning.

– Quamer F

TESTIMONIALS

In 2020 I was in a class Rodney taught for Financial Freedom, I have learned in the past four years you can't out give God, He will always bless you for your obedience and faithfulness. I have personally seen it time after time. Before Rodney's teachings I couldn't make it through the month on my fixed income now God always provides in one way or another. One of my most recent blessings was I received an unexpected check from my insurance company a week before my car needed repair and the check was enough to cover the repair. This is just one example of God's blessings over the last four years since learning about Financial Freedom.

Always be a cheerful, faithful giver and watch what God can do in your life also.

If you put these biblical principles to work in your heart and finances, it does work! Although so many of us struggle to get by day to day God will always come through. I've been applying my giving with a different perspective these last few months and just when I least expected it, a miracle check came in the mail. Thank You, Jesus, and thank you, Rodney, for sharing.

What I learned from this is when we obey God's leading, He is faithful to provide, He shows up and shows off! God put the resources into my hands that were never meant to be mine; I was simply the vessel he could channel his resources through. Now whenever God blessed me with an unexpected increase I ask Him if it is meant for me or if I am only the channel to answer someone else's prayer. These financial principles I learned and am applying not only are bringing me closer to Financial Freedom, they are helping me mature in my walk with Christ, bless others and see personal goals and dreams come closer to fulfillment. Giving God all praise for His faithfulness.

This teaching has helped me see finances in a whole new light and gave me faith that it's still possible to plan for retirement even after 40.

Thanks to Rodney's teaching and his insightful knowledge on Financial Freedom, I've successfully aligned my finances, learned to save, budget effectively, and even boost my credit score by 100 points! Rodney's practical advice on financial management has been a game-changer for me.

About the Author

A little about me: I am currently a bank manager since 2019 and have been working in banking since 2008. I studied at Liberty University and Bethany Theological Seminary where I studied accounting and biblical studies and became ordained in 2008. I am a father of two and an entrepreneur. In my free time, I enjoy trading and investing in the stock market and spending time with my friends and family. I have been teaching financial literacy since 2020 through church groups and have personally experienced the life-changing impact it has made in their lives. I wrote this book as a living testimony of what God can do. He changed my life, and He can change yours too.

Endnotes

1   "Living paycheck to paycheck statistics." Jason Steele and Erik Martin. Published September 18, 2023. *Bankrate* <https://www.bankrate.com/finance/credit-cards/living-paycheck-to-paycheck-statistics/>

2   "Coping with Financial Stress." Lawrence Robinson and Melinda Smith. Accessed June 11, 2024. *HelpGuide* <https://www.helpguide.org/articles/stress/coping-with-financial-stress.htm>

3   "Confessions for Reaping a Harvest by Jerry Savelle." Kenneth Copeland Ministries. Published January 28, 2019. YouTube <https://www.youtube.com/watch?v=sr_myYzDb-o>

4   "7 Stats Highlighting How Much Money Americans Waste on Nonessentials — Why We Do It and How To Stop." Dawn Allcot. Published August 31, 2023. *Yahoo Finance* <https://finance.yahoo.com/news/7-stats-highlighting-much-money-182939795.html>

5   "Here's Why 82% of Americans Use Credit Cards." Lyle Daly. Published February 6, 2024. *The Ascent* *<https://www.fool.com/the-ascent/credit-cards/articles/heres-why-82-of-americans-use-credit-cards/>*

GOD'S FORMULA FOR FINANCIAL FREEDOM

6   "Nearly Half Have Less Than $500 in Savings: How To Build Up Your Balance in 2024." Jacob Wade. Published February 5, 2024. *GOBankingRates* <https://www.gobankingrates.com/saving-money/savings-advice/nearly-half-have-less-than-500-in-savings-how-to-build-up-your-balance/>

7   "My Hope is Built on Nothing Less." Accessed July 8, 2024. *Hymnary* <https://hymnary.org/text/my_hope_is_built_on_nothing_less>

Printed in the USA
CPSIA information can be obtained
at www.ICGtesting.com
CBHW070111220924
14609CB00019B/1255